Cromosys Publication

Teach Yourself Microsoft Excel

NIRANJAN JHA SHOWMAN

Founder - Niranjan Jha Showman

Education and Technology Research Center

Patankar Park, Nallasopara (W), Mumbai. +91-9561450045

Education, Technology, Publication, Healthcare, Newsmedia, Realtor, Filmmaking

www.facebook.com/cromosys

+91-9561450045
Learn Advanced Skills
And Get Job Instantly
GERMAN
Python
FRENCH
C++
SPANISH
Java
ENGLISH
HTML5
RUSSIAN
CSS
JavaScript
Cromosys
Education and Technology Research Center
Nallasopara (W), Mumbai

Learn Web Programming
Demo-Class Free
HTML
CSS
React
JavaScript
Typescript
Bootstrap
Cromosys
20 Years of Experience
Nallasopara (W), Mumbai
+91-9561450045

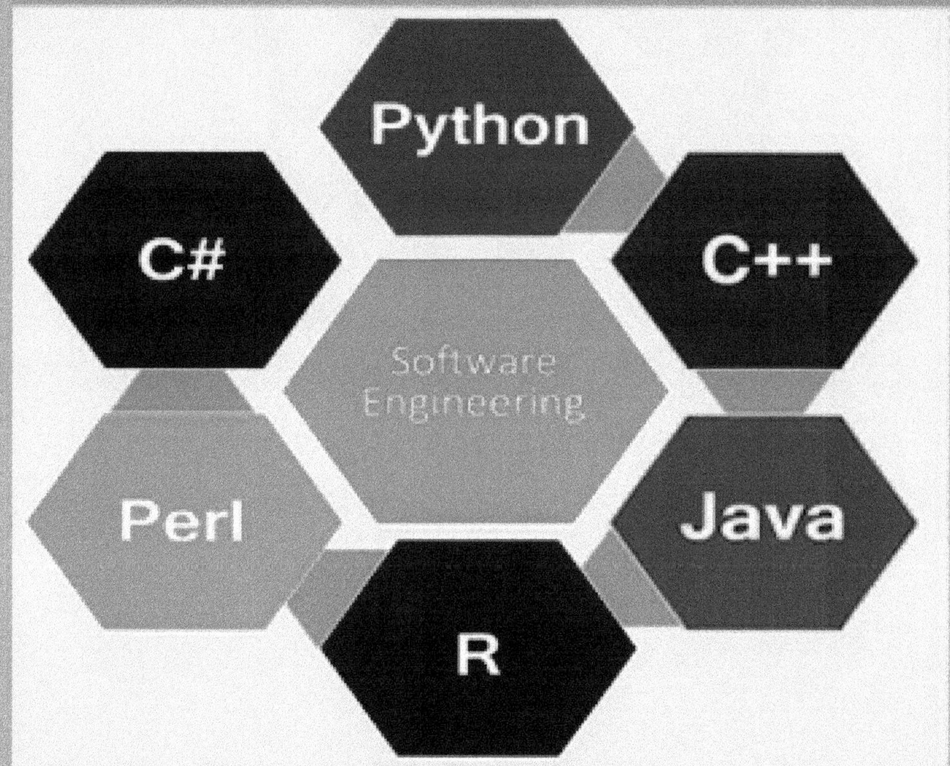

+91-9561450045
Learn Software Engineering
Demo-Class Free
Python
C#
C++
Software Engineering
Perl
Java
R
Cromosys
20 Years of Experience
Nallasopara (W), Mumbai
+91-9561450045

25 Years of Experience
Learn Visual Multimedia
Animation VFX
Movie Editing
Game Development
Cromosys
+91-9561450045
Education and Technology Research Center
Nallasopara (W), Mumbai
www.facebook.com/cromosys

Jobs Available
For Candidates Who Know

German

French

Spanish

Vacancy in Germany, France, Spain
For Hospitality, Engineering, IT Sector
With Free Visa, Airfare and Accommodation

Cromosys
Education and Technology Research Centre
Nallasopara (W), Mumbai
+91-9561450045
20 Years of Experience

+91-9561450045
Foreign Languages Institute
German, French, Spanish
Basic and Advanced - All Levels
3 x 6 = 18 Courses
FRANCHISE
Business Offer
Teaching Materials Provided
We have 1 Million Students Globally
Great Income Assured
Global Exposure
Cromosys
20 Years of Experience
Nallasopara (W), Mumbai
+91-9561450045

Book: Teach Yourself Microsoft Excel
Author: Niranjan Jha Showman
Publisher: Cromosys Publication
ISBN: Acquired
Date: 2022
Category: Computer Education

Preface

Some people say that Microsoft Excel is so easy that there is no need of any book to learn this program. What they say is right, but do you know one thing? They have never known how big Microsoft Excel is, and what are the advanced commands associated with this application. There are hundreds of advanced commands, which after you learn, help you work with this application efficiently. And so, we have explained about all the basic and advanced commands of Excel 2013, and have given the steps with pictures in this book. Cromosys Publication's **Teach Yourself Microsoft Excel** book is an optimal quality guide to the beginners and advanced learners of Microsoft Excel 2013 and further versions. We are the leading book publisher of languages and technology. Our research and education center working for last fifteen years has made tremendous efforts to simplify the learning of Microsoft Excel, and so we assure you that this book will walk you through in the simplest way in your entire course of learning, and will make you a master of Microsoft Excel application in just one month of time. This all-inclusive book provides you with in-depth knowledge of Excel with various steps and examples. An easy-to-understand, step-by-step approach, supplemented with practical implementation and many real-life screenshots are some of the distinguishing features of the book. Microsoft Excel is a program that is specifically designed to organize data in tables and to analyze the tabulated data. Excel is the world's most widely used spreadsheet program, and is a part of the Microsoft Office suite. The lessons of this book conceived and prepared by us will help you start learning from real basic making your move amazing, astonishing, and exhilarating for you. It's cool, simple, and sublime!

Niranjan Showman, the author of this and fifty other books published online, is the coiner, founder, and owner of Cromosys Corporation. His dedication in technological and linguistic research is significantly known to millions of people around the world. This book is the creation of his avowed determination to make the learning of Microsoft Excel easy to the people. After you install the application on your system, you just have to follow the instructions of this book doing the same on your computer, and you will see that you are quickly learning everything. Just an hour of practice per day, and in a month of time you'll get a lot of knowledge, tips and tricks to work with this software. This is an unmatchable unique book of its kind that guarantees your success. The lessons are magnificently powerful to bring you into the arena of tabulated data-analyzing. With the industrial growth from the year 2014, the accurate and profound knowledge of this software has influenced millions of minds; therefore we conceived the idea of making this book a guideline to those who want to be perfect in this application starting from real basic.

Cromosys education system is intelligently dedicated to our avid and passionate readers, predominantly acknowledging and appreciating the fact that they are on the path of making a career in the respective domains. Each Cromosys book is designed to ensure that in addition to gaining the requisite theoretical knowledge, the readers gain sufficient hands-on practice and practical knowhow to master the nitty-gritty of the profession. Since Microsoft has revolutionized the working experience on personal computers with its office automation applications, due to the interactive user-interface and simplicity of use, Microsoft Excel gained popularity very quickly. Excel is popular because of its versatility. It performs numerical calculations, and is very useful for non-numerical applications. Excel also provides the facility to covert the worksheet data into various charts, such as bar, pie, 2-dimensional, and 3-dimensional, to understand the worksheet data easily. With this application, it is easier than ever to efficiently create a wide range of business and personal documents. It includes many desktop publishing features that you can use to enhance the appearance of documents to make them more appealing and readable. Microsoft Excel 2013 has been completely redesigned to make it user friendly so that even a novice user can work on it efficiently.

Cromosys, our education and technology research center, saving human efforts from being wasted, is committed to help you gain profound and contemporary knowledge. The world growing with density has brought enormous opportunity to computer professionals irrespective of their geographical boundaries. We strongly believe that this book is useful to all who work on Microsoft Excel. After you start the lesson, you don't need to worry about anything but just follow each and every step carefully. This book is designed to fulfill the instant need of learners in a very economical way, as it is easy to find on Internet and affordable to buy and share. Cromosys, our path-breaking pioneer training institute for Computer Courses, English Speaking, Foreign Languages, and Competition Coaching, is dedicated to enlightening human mind with educational endeavors, and we are doing the same for last successful fifteen years. And recently we have come up with 'Worldwide Online Teaching System' for languages and technology. We not only hope but believe that your success is in your hand, as this book will take you miles ahead in your expectation. We always respect the views and comments of readers, so for any communication with regards to assistance, enquiry or collaboration, we are always there at your reach as it helps us improve our quality.

Niranjan Jha Showman
Founder: Cromosys Corporation
Web: facebook.com/cromosys
Contact no.   +91-9561450045
Email address: cromosys@yahoo.com

Books by the same author:
Teach Yourself Tally, Teach Yourself Microsoft Word, Teach Yourself Adobe Premiere Pro, Teach Yourself Adobe Flash, Teach Yourself Adobe Dreamweaver, Teach Yourself Autodesk Maya, Teach Yourself Autodesk 3ds Max, English Voice Accent and Pronunciation, English Word Power, English Dictionary of Modern Slang, Teach Yourself Spanish, Teach Yourself French, Teach Yourself German

Cromosys
Education and Technology Research Center
Education, Technology, Publication, Healthcare, Realtor, Filmmaking
Nallasopara (W), Mumbai, India

Caution: All the writing works that include all the educational, non-educational books, novels, and articles of the author Niranjan Jha, are the registered contents of Online Digital Services and also published contents of his registered magazine FACE OFF - Inventing Truth, which carries registration no. MAHENG12112/13/1/2009-TC and the endorsement no. 3244 28/5/2009 with the Ministry of Information and Broadcasting, Govt. of India. Any plagiarism in this regard will attract strict legal action. Any further publication of any of his books requires his written permission. Copyright certificate of this book is attached at the end of this book.

Lesson 1
Introduction

The interface of Microsoft Excel 2013 is easier to learn because it is more logical and visual. The first thing you notice about this application is its new look, which is very different from its older versions. The menu bar and toolbar user interface has been replaced with a new tab and ribbon interface. Excel users may have probably noticed that the menu system becomes more complicated with every new version. To solve this problem, a new ribbon interface is introduced in this application. Over the time, the most common complaint about Excel was the small size of its worksheets. Excel 2013 comes with a worksheet having 1,048,576 rows and 16,384 columns.

The chapter begins by showing you how to start the Microsoft Excel 2013 application. Next, you learn to work with spreadsheet, after this you learn the basics of spreadsheet. In addition, you explore the Excel interface. Towards the end of the chapter, you learn to close the workbook and quit the Microsoft Excel application. Let's begin with opening the Microsoft Excel application.

Starting Microsoft Excel 2013

Now we are going to open Microsoft Excel application. Perform the following steps on your computer to start Microsoft Excel:

1. Click the **Start** button at the bottom-left side on your desktop.

2. Select **All Programs**, and click **Microsoft Office**.

3. Click **Microsoft Excel 2013** in the Microsoft Office list. It opens a new Excel worksheet on the window, as shown in picture 1.1.

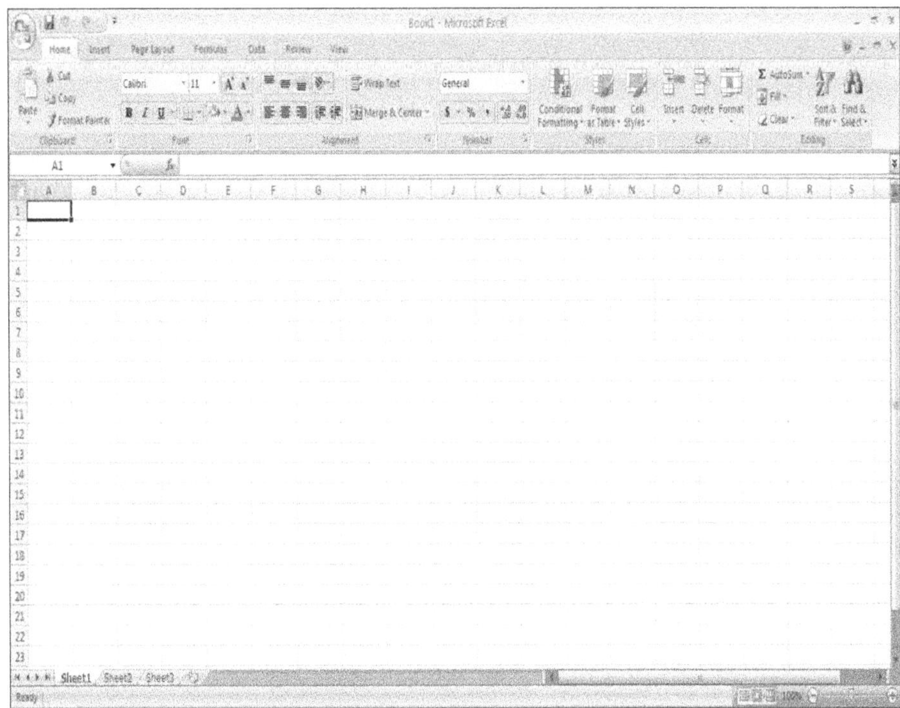

Picture 1.1

In Microsoft Excel 2013, all the menu and toolbars have been replaced with the ribbon which makes your work easy. As an Excel application is based upon spreadsheet, you must understand what a spreadsheet is all about.

Working with Spreadsheet

Spreadsheet is a simple worksheet consisting of rows and columns for entering data. Spreadsheets are used for doing various tasks, such as performing calculations, recalculating results (if any data stored in them is changed), creating financial reports, and comparing reports. A very useful feature of the spreadsheet is its ability to create groups. It helps you to establish relationship between two or more sets of data and to easily understand the trend of data change.

A report card of a student or a ledger created to maintain bank accounts are some common examples of a spreadsheet. While report cards of students are manual spreadsheets, ledgers can be maintained both manually or electronically. An electronic spreadsheet is similar to a paper spreadsheet; however, it is created on a computer. As compared to manual spreadsheets, it takes less time in preparing and updating electronic spreadsheets. Let's consider the manual spreadsheet prepared by a teacher based on the students' marks in various subjects, as shown in picture 1.2.

CLASS REPORT					
		RITA	DAVID	CHARLES	KEVIN
SUBJECT	MAX MARKS				
ENGLISH	100	70	80	72	67
MATHS	100	57	90	80	82
SCIENCE	100	79	79	85	92
SST	100	60	72	60	87
DRAWING	100	67	80	70	80
G.K. GR.	A+	B	A+	B+	A+
TOTAL	600	$398^{1/2}$	$477^{1/2}$	434	488
% (AGE)		66.30%	79.50%	72.33%	81.33%

Picture 1.2

Now suppose, some change is required in the English marks of Kevin. In this case, resetting Kevin's marks would be tedious and time-consuming as his total marks and the percentage would need to be changed manually. However, if we change Kevin's English marks in an electronic spreadsheet, his total marks and percentage will get recalculated automatically. You learn more about various useful features of electronic spreadsheets when you work in Excel; however, let's first get a basic idea about a cell and its role and significance in a spreadsheet.

Cell and Cell Address

A spreadsheet consists of **rows** and **columns**. The intersection of a row and column creates a **cell**, into which you can enter data. Each cell has a unique cell address, which indentifies the location of that cell. A particular cell is addressed by combining the column letter and row number. Cell addresses starting with row numbers, like 3B or 10A, are invalid cell addresses. In picture 1.3 below, **A1** is the address of the cell that is formed at the intersection of column **A** and row **1**:

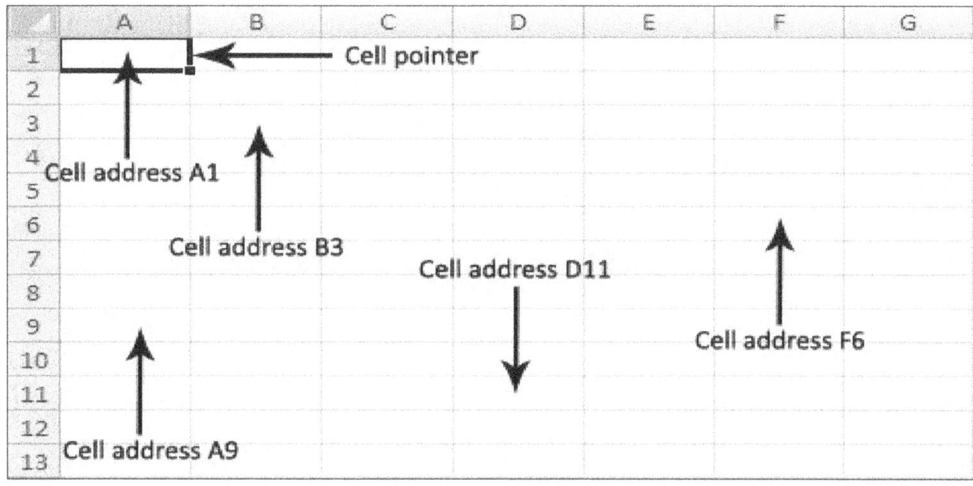

Picture 1.3

Cell Pointer

As you know, in Microsoft Word, when mouse-pointer is clicked inside a document, a blinking cursor gets displayed. However, in the Microsoft Excel spreadsheet, when the mouse-pointer is clicked at any place, a **cell-pointer** appears. The currently active cell is the one on which the cell-pointer is placed. In a new sheet, as shown in picture 1.3, the cell pointer by default is positioned at cell address **A1**.

Labels and Values

You can enter various types of data in an Excel sheet, such as text, numbers, formulas, or special characters. **Value** is a number on which calculations are done using formulas. Whenever an entry starts with +, -, . sign or a digit, Microsoft Excel considers it to be a value.

Label is any text entry that contains alphabet or non-numeric characters, such as # and &. Some examples of labels are Accounts, #4, and Monthly-expenses. Entries containing an alphabet or letter – even if they start with a number are considered text entries, such as 24 Linking Road and 4th. The table in picture 1.4 provides a better idea of labels and values.

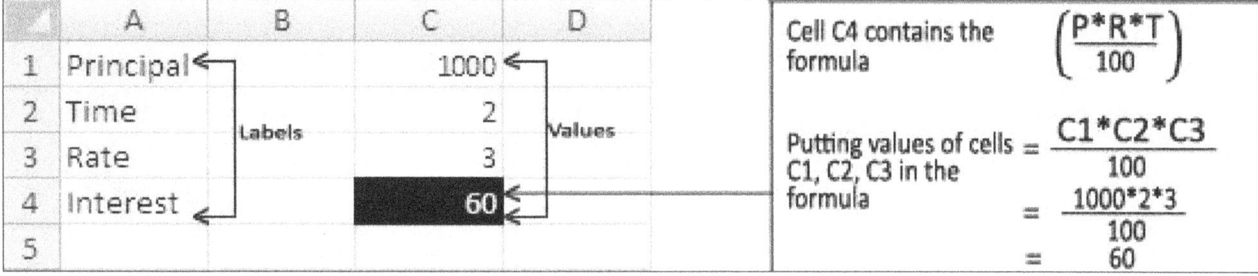

Picture 1.4: Idea of Labels and Values

Formulas

In an Excel spreadsheet, you can carry out any mathematical or analytical operation on the cell data by using a formula. For example, cell **C4** contains the formula that calculates the interest (Picture 1.4 cell). Cell **C1** contains principal (P), **C2** contains time (T), and **C3** contains rate (R). Therefore, according to the formula of **C4**, the interest calculated is 60.

Functions

Formulas that are in-built into a spreadsheet are called **functions**. Formulas in cells **B6**, **C6**, **D6** calculate the sum, the average, and the maximum number of marks, respectively awarded to the students in different subjects, as shown in picture 1.5. The computations appearing in the picture 1.5 are the result of formulas prepared and executed in a spreadsheet:

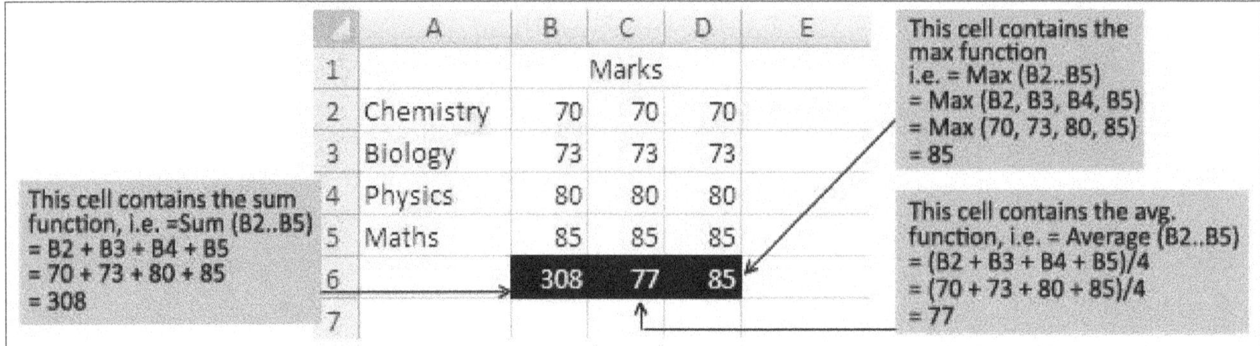

Picture 1.5: Result of Formulas

What-if Analysis

The **What-if Analysis** feature of Excel 2013 allows you to see how the change in values or data of one or more cells affects the outcome of formulas in the worksheet. For example, if Rita's marks in Science are to be changed to 90 from 79 (picture 1.2), the using the What-if Analysis feature, you can quickly find out what would be her total marks and how much would be the increase in her percentage.

Automatic Recalculation

A major drawback of a manual spreadsheet is that if any data in it changes, you have to redo all the calculations affected by that change. However, an electronic spreadsheet of Microsoft Excel automatically perform all such calculations for your. All you have to do is to just change the data and the rest is taken care of by the spreadsheet. The Automatic Recalculation feature proves very useful in What-if Analysis.

To understand how Excel carries out the automatic recalculation, let's consider an example in which Column B contains Salary of a person as well as expenses incurred by him on Goods, Rent, and Travel (picture 1.6). The Total column displays the sum of expenses on Goods, Rent, and Travel. The Savings column in picture 1.6 are calculated as the difference between Salary and Total that is 2800 and 2050, respectively.

	A	B	C
1	Salary	2800	
2,	Goods	800	
3	Rent	1000	
4	Travel	250	
5	Total	2050	
6	Savings	750	

This cell contains the formula
= Salary - Total
= B1 - B5
= 2800 - 2050
= 750

This cell contains the formula
= Goods + Rent + Travel
= B2 + B3 + B4
= 2050

Picture 1.6: Calculate the Difference between Salary and Total

Now, in the next picture 1.7, if the amount spent on Goods is increased from 800 to 1000, the values in the Total as well as in Savings columns changes. It should be noted that the formula applied in both the tables is the same. Microsoft Excel replaces the old value of Goods with a new value and recalculates the Total and Savings. Picture 1.7 shows the Total changes from 2050 to 2250 and Savings change from 750 to 550.

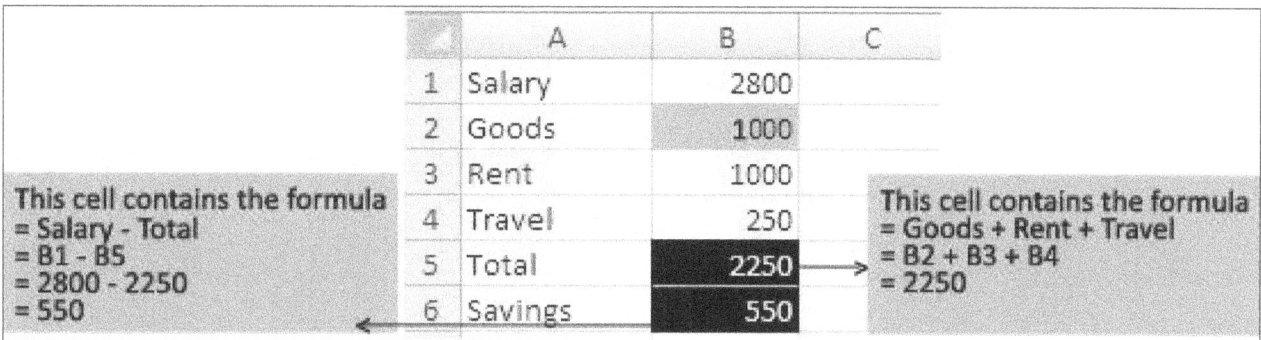

Picture 1.7: Replace the Old Value with New Value

Format a Spreadsheet

A spreadsheet can be designed in a number of formats. Basically, number formatting is concerned with how the data in a spreadsheet appears on the screen. The data in a cell may also be right aligned, left aligned, or centered.

Exploring Microsoft Excel

The user interface (UI) of Microsoft Excel 2013 is very different from its previous versions. When you start Microsoft Excel, a sheet appears (picture 1.1). Now, let's have a look at the major components of the UI of Microsoft Excel 2013.

Office button

The Office button is present at the left-most upper corner of the worksheet. When you click on this button, a dropdown menu appears containing many options for working with a document. You need to use this button many times while working in Microsoft Excel. In technical terms, you can say that it is the replacement of the File menu, as it has almost the same option that used to be there in the File menu, such as new, open, save, and print. On the lower portion, there are two buttons named Excel Options and Exit Excel. When you click on the Excel Options button, a dialog box appears using which you can make changes in various features. On the other hand, the Exit Excel button is used to exit from Microsoft Excel.

Quick Access Toolbar

The Quick Access toolbar is placed adjacent to the Office button. A toolbar holds commonly used Excel commands. Clicking the Customize Quick Access Toolbar button displays a dropdown list containing some excel commands, such as Undo, Redo, Save, and New. The dropdown list also contains the More Command option. On clicking this option, a dialog box appears that you can use to add or remove buttons on the Quick Access toolbar.

Title Bar

The Title bar is present on the top of the worksheet, adjacent to the Quick Access toolbar. The name of the program and current workbook is displayed on the title bar. All window programs have a title bar. It also holds some control buttons that you can use to modify the window.

Minimize, Maximize, and Close Buttons

Minimize, Maximize, and Close buttons are present on the right-most upper corner of the window. Starting from the corner, if we move towards the left side, then the buttons appear in the sequence close, maximize/restore, and minimize. The functions of the all these three buttons are different from each other.

Minimize Button: There are two minimize buttons, present one below the other. Clicking on the lower button minimizes the current window while clicking on the upper button minimizes the whole application.

Maximize Button: There are two maximize buttons same as that of the minimize buttons. The lower button is used to increase the workbook window's size to fill Excel's complete workplace. If the window is already maximized, clicking the button will minimize the current window. On the other hand, clicking on the upper button results in the maximization of the whole application and vice versa.

Close Buttons: Once again, there are two close buttons on the Excel window. The lower button is used to close the active workbook window while the upper is used to close the main Excel window or application.

Exploring Menus

Menu is a list of commands or options from which you can choose only one at a time. You can choose any time from the menu by highlighting it and then pressing enter key, or by simply pointing to the item with a mouse and clicking mouse button.

Command driven system is different from a menu driven program, in which you must explicitly enter the command rather than choosing from a list of possible commands. Menu driven systems are easier and simpler to learn but are generally not as flexible as command driven systems. In Office 2013, menus are arranged horizontally and are also known as tabs. When you click on a tab, the ribbon changes and the commands present in it also change accordingly, depending upon which tab is selected. The ribbon is arranged into a group of related commands and is displayed below the title bar. The tabs present in Microsoft Excel 2013 are as follows:

Home: Contains the basic clipboard commands, formatting commands, style commands, command to insert and delete rows and columns, and editing commands. This tab also provides commands for changing the font-color, style, or size of the entered data in the worksheet. Picture 1.8 shows the Home tab of Microsoft Excel:

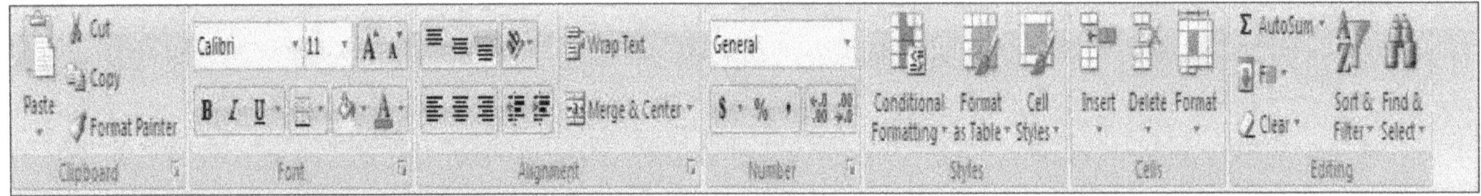

Picture 1.8 shows the group of Home tab and its purposes

Groups of Home tab

Clipboard	This group contains the commands to cut/copy, and paste data from one location to another. The format painter in this group allows you to copy and apply formatting features.
Font	Contains commands to change the font face, size, style, and color. All the options to make necessary changes to the appearance of font are present in this group.
Alignment	Allows two types of alignments in Excel 2013 – horizontal and Vertical. Different commands related to both the types are present in this group.
Number	Contains various commands to make changes in the values present in a cell. The values may be currency, text, date, or time.
Styles	Contains commands for many formatting styles to change the look of a worksheet such as Conditional formatting style, format as table, and cell styles.
Cells	Contains commands to insert, delete, and format a cell. In the format cell command, you can format the cell by changing the cells property such as size and visibility. You can also change the color of a tab using this command in Home tab.
Editing	This group contains commands for sorting and filtering. Commands related to find and replace are also present in this group.

Insert: Allows you to insert a table, picture, clipart, chart, word art, symbol, header and footer, and different shapes in the worksheet. Picture 1.9 below shows the Insert tab with its groups in Microsoft Excel 2013:

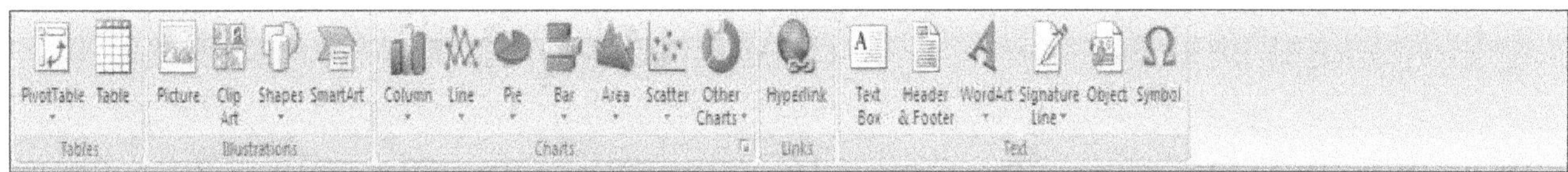

Picture 1.9 shows the groups of Insert tab and its purposes

Groups of Insert tab

Tables	Contains commands to insert a simple table, pivot table, and pivot chart on a worksheet.
Illustrations	Contains commands to insert pictures, clipart, shapes, and smart arts on a worksheet.
Charts	Contains commands to insert different types of charts in a worksheet.
Links	Contains commands to insert hyperlinks in a worksheet.
Text	Contains commands to insert textboxes, word art, object, symbol, and headers and footers in a worksheet.

Page Layout: Contains all the commands that affect the overall appearance of a worksheet. These commands are arranged in various groups for easy access. Some of the commands present in this tab are themes, page size, background, effects, and align. Various settings related to printing the worksheet, such as print area and print titles are also present in this tab. Picture 2.0 shows the Page Layout tab of Microsoft Excel:

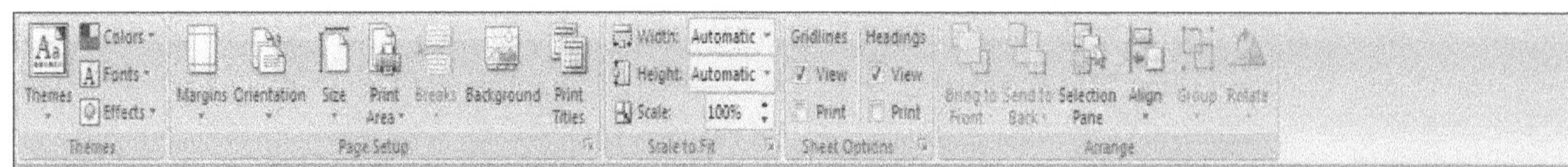

Picture 2.0 shows the groups of Page Layout tab and its purposes

Groups of Page Layout tab

Themes Contains commands and options to change the fonts, fonts colors, and color scheme for a worksheet.

Page Setup Contains commands to change setting of a page, such as Margins, Orientation, Size, Print Area, Breaks, Background and Print Titles.

Scale to Fit Contains commands/options to change the width and height of printing area in a worksheet.

Sheet Options Contains commands to show gridlines and headings on the worksheet. Command to print those gridlines and headings is also present in the group.

Arrange Contains commands/options to change the arrangement of objects placed in a worksheet. You can use this group in Excel to change the alignment of objects, rotate objects in specific directions, and group different objects into single object.

Formulas: Allows you to insert a formula, name a range, and access the formula auditing tools. This tab controls how Excel performs calculations and gives results. Excel provides the various formulas, such as logical, financial, lookup and reference, and text and math to perform calculations. Picture 2.1 shows the Formulas tab of Microsoft Excel:

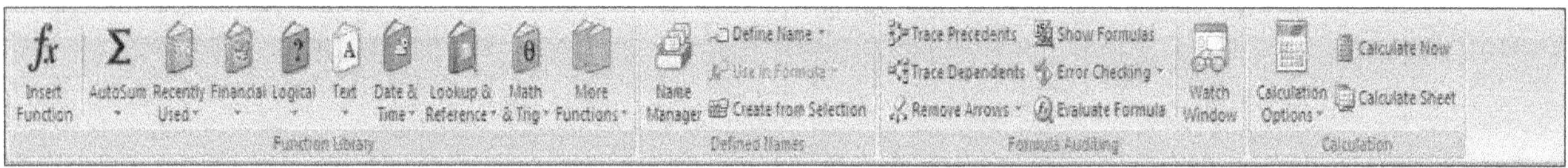

Picture 2.1 shows the group of Formulas tab and its purposes

Groups of Formulas tab

Function and Library Contains commands to various categories of function. When you click any of the dropdown buttons of this group, you will find that the functions are subdivided in different parts.

Defined Names Allows you to create and organize names of formulas, tables, and cell ranges used in a worksheet. You can use the names to find error values as well as help for other calculations.

Formula Auditing Contains commands/options to audit a formula for error and view its precedents and dependents.

Calculation Contains commands/options to change the calculation mode of Microsoft Excel. Besides automatic calculation mode, you can set manual calculation mode to perform calculation only after clicking the necessary button. Using this group, you can restrict calculation for data tables.

Data: Allows you to import data from external sources, such as Access, SQL server, or Web. Various data related commands and tools are present in this tab. The Sort & Filter option is available in this section, with the help of which you can sort the data present in your worksheet. Picture 2.2 shows the Data tab of Microsoft Excel:

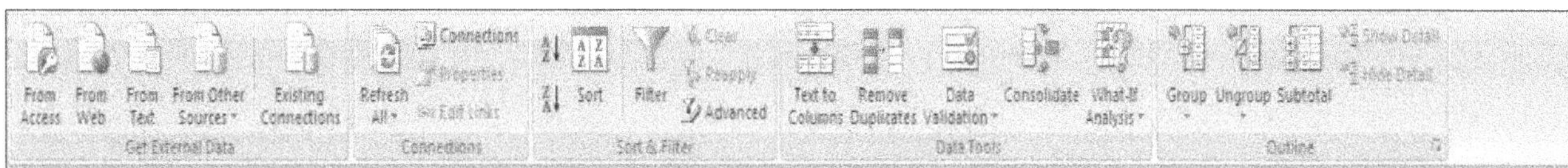

Picture 2.2 shows the group of Data tab and its purposes

Groups of Data tab

Get External Data	Contains commands to import data from some external sources, such as Access, Web, or from some other source.
Connections	Contains commands to make connections with other files or data present in the same computer or some other computer.
Sort Filter	Contains commands to sort and filter the data present on the worksheet.
Data Tools	Contains commands to remove duplicate values from the worksheet. Some other commands, such as what-if analysis are also present in this group.
Outline	Contains commands to group or ungroup rows and columns of a worksheet. Command to find subtotal is also present in this group.

Review: This tab contains various tools related to checking the spelling, translating words, adding comments, and protecting the workbook. A user may want to protect his data from unauthorized access. In such a case, he can make use of the Protect Sheet and Workbook option available on the Review tab. Picture 2.3 shows the Review tab of Microsoft Excel:

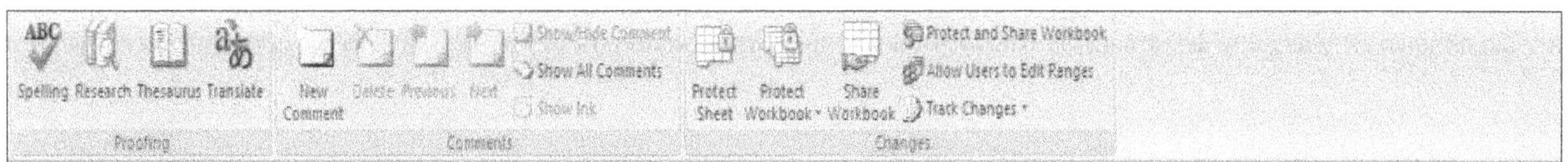

Picture 2.3 shows a group of Review tab and its purposes

Groups of Review tab

Proofing	Contains commands to spell check, research, and translate. The Spell check command is used to check the spelling of the selected data.
Comments	Contains commands to add, edit, and delete comments in a cell. Commands to move on next and previous comments are also present under this group.
Changes	Contains commands to protect, unprotect, and share the worksheet and workbook.

View: In this tab, the commands related to page view or layout is present. In the window group, various commands are present that are used to split the worksheet. One more command named hide is also present, which is used to hide the current window so that it cannot be seen. To bring the hidden window back, an unhide button is also present there. Picture 2.4 shows the View tab of Microsoft Excel:

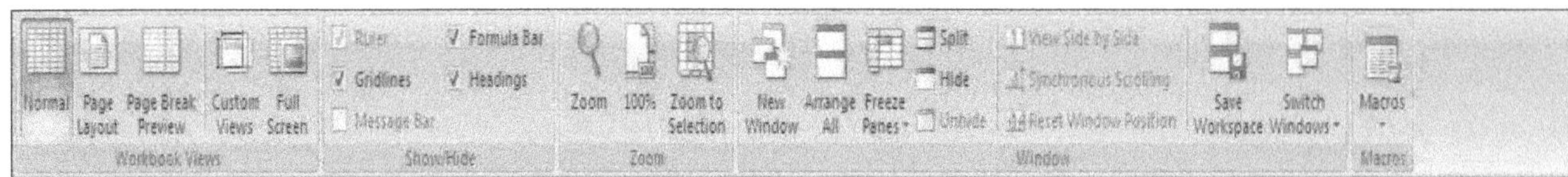

Picture 2.4 shows a group of View tab and its purposes

Groups of View tab

Workbook views	Contains commands to view the worksheet in different ways, such as normal, custom, page layout, and full screen view.
Show/Hide	Contains commands to show common toolbars, such as ruler, formula bar, gridlines, and headings in the Excel window.
Zoom	Contains commands to zoom in the worksheet. This command zooms the selected region or the whole worksheet at a time.
Window	Contains commands/options to view windows in different views. Besides viewing, you can split a window into two parts – switch to another workbook or save a workbook as new workspace for future.
Macros	Contains commands/options that allow you to view macros present in the workbook as well as record a new macro.

Formula Bar

Formula bar is present below the ribbon tab and above the work area of the worksheet. Formula bar displays the data or formula stored in the active cell. It can also be used to enter or edit a formula, a function, or a data present in a cell. When you enter any data or formula in a cell, it appears in the formula bar. When you click with mouse on the formula bar, an X and a check mark appear. You can click on the check icon to confirm editing and X to leave editing.

Work Area

The place, where we enter the data or record and perform various operations, is known as work area. A work area consists of rows, columns, and cells. Now we are going to discuss about all the terms, one by one:

- **Rows:** Allows you to start numbers from 1 to 1,048,576 – one for each row in the worksheet. You can choose a row number to select the entire row of cells. In Excel 2003, there were 65,536 rows; however, in Excel 2007, there are 1,048,576 rows.
- **Columns:** Allows you to start letter ranges from A to IXFD – one for each of the 16,384 columns in the worksheet. You can click a column heading to select an entire column of cells. In Excel 2003, there were 256 columns; however, in Excel 2007, there are 16,384 columns.
- **Cell:** Refers to the intersection of a row and column. For example, a cell located where column D and row 9 intersects is called as D9. The active cell has a dark border around it, which indicates your current position on the worksheet. The data you type is inserted in the active cell.
- **Cell Addressing:** Provides the location of the cell in a spreadsheet. A cell address consists of a column letter followed by a row number. They are combined to make the address of the selected cell. It was known as name box in previous versions.

Scroll Bars

The grey bars present at the right side and at the bottom of the worksheet on the window frame that allow the user to move up-down and left-right through the viewable area of the worksheet are known as scroll bars. You can also use it when you need to ask for a value, which falls within a certain range. Using scroll bars, you can quickly access the worksheet from up-down or left-right. There are two types of scroll bars – Horizontal and Vertical.

- **Horizontal Scrollbar:** Enables the user to move from left right on the worksheet or on a section of the window.
- **Vertical Scrollbar:** Enables the user to move from up down on a worksheet or on a section of the window.

Sheets Tab

The Sheet tab is present near the horizontal scrollbar and represents various worksheets in the workbook. A workbook can have any number of worksheets, and each worksheet has its different name displayed in the Sheet tab. By default, each new workbook has three sheets. You can add more worksheets to a workbook by just clicking the Insert Worksheet button, which exists next to the last sheet tab.

Status Bar and Navigation Pane

The Status bar exists below the sheet tab. It is divided into sections, each of which shows different information. Its main job is to display the information about the current state of the window. Statuses of the num lock, caps lock, and scroll lock keys are also displayed on the status bar. You can also customize the information displayed on the status bar by right-clicking on it. Navigation pane is not visible directly. To make it visible, you have to click on the save or open button. A dialog box appears containing various options, one of which is navigation pane. It exists below the caption save in, and is widely used for Quick Access to the locations where you want to save or from where you want to open the current document. When you click on any item in a navigation pane, a file or folder related to that item appears on the right side of the navigation pane.

Exploring the Excel Options

When you click the **Office button> Excel Options** at the bottom, it opens the Excel Options dialog box on the screen. The dialog box has two sections – left and right. The left section contains many lists of categories while the right section contains various options related to the list of categories. By default, **Popular** list of category and options related to it will be displayed on the dialog box. You can make changes in various settings related to font and languages in this category.

When you click on any other category, then options related to that appear on the right side of the dialog box. Using this dialog box, a user can choose the file format from a given list of categories. You can also change the default file location. You can also set time for an auto recovery on the information which recovers your information.

In this section, you have explored menus in Excel and learned about the Excel options. Now we are going to learn about closing the workbook and quitting Excel.

Closing the Workbook and Quitting Excel

If you have completed the work on the worksheet and want to close the sheet, you can do so by performing the following steps:

1. Click the **Office button** to open a dropdown list.

2. Click the **Close** option in the dropdown list.

If more than one page is opened in the Excel window, you have to click on the Close button of every page. But when you want to exit from the main window of Excel, you need to click the Office button and then the **Exit Excel** button.

Lesson 2
Preparing the First Excel Worksheet

A worksheet consists of rows and columns that allow you to enter data in a tabular format. After entering data in an Excel worksheet, you can perform various tasks, such as sorting data, performing calculations, and printing a worksheet. In Excel, data can also be represented in form of charts, such as Column, Line, Pie, and Bar. You can also insert different illustrations, such as Picture, Clip Art, Shapes, and Smart Art. Excel imports data from different external sources, such as Microsoft Access, SQL Server, XML Data, and Web. Any change in a cell affects the entire result and sometimes generates an error. For an effective view of a worksheet, you can apply different fonts, colors, and alignments.

In this lesson, you learn how to enter data in a worksheet by selecting cells, using the cut, copy, and paste commands and then performing spelling-check and auto correct utility on the data. Next, you learn to format cells by adjusting rows and columns, setting the currency symbol, decimal places, date and time, setting the font and highlighting the cells, and setting cell alignment and orientation of a cell. Towards the middle of the lesson, you learn to format a worksheet by applying margins, inserting header and footer, customizing header and footer, applying a background for worksheet, renaming a worksheet, adding color to the Sheet tab, adding new worksheet, and selecting the center page alignment for the worksheet. Further, you learn to save a workbook in different formats, assigning a password to the worksheet, and unprotecting a worksheet. At the end of the lesson, you learn to prepare a worksheet for printing by adding print title, row and column heading, and gridlines, inserting breaks, viewing the print preview of the worksheet, and printing a worksheet.

Entering Data in Worksheet

Data can be entered in a worksheet in two ways, first is manually and second is automatically. In manually, the data is entered by the user. In automatically, the data is imported from some other systems or sources, such as Access, SQL Server or from Web. In Automatic data entry, you can enter any type of data, such as numeric, text, date, or time in one cell, in many cells, or on more than one worksheet at a time. A worksheet can also contains charts, diagrams, pictures, buttons, and other objects. Now perform the following steps to enter data manually:

1. **Open** a blank Excel worksheet.
2. Click cell **A1** and type **Branch Wise Salary for July 2014**.
3. Click cell **A2** and type **Emp Name** as a column heading.

4. Click cell **B2** and type **Branch**.
5. Click cell **C2** and type **Department**.
6. Click cell **D2** and type **Leave**.
7. Click cell **E2** and type **Salary**.
8. Click cell **F2** and type **Salary Drawn On**.

All the headings required for salary sheet have been entered on the sheet, as shown in picture 2.5. Now you have to enter the values required for the salary sheet.

	A	B	C	D	E	F	G
1	Branch Wise Salary for July 2014						
2	Emp Name	Branch	Department	Leave	Salary	Salary Drawn On	
3							
4							
5							
6							
7							
8							

Picture 2.5

9. Click cell **A3** and **enter** value for <u>Emp Name</u>. In our case, we enter the name of three employees.
10. Click cell **B3** and **enter** value for <u>Branch</u>. In our case, we type the name of the branch.
11. Click cell **C3** and **enter** value for <u>Department</u>.
12. Click cell **D3** and **enter** value for <u>Leave</u>.
13. Click cell **E3** and **enter** value for <u>Salary</u>.
14. Click cell **F3** and **enter** value for <u>Salary Drawn On</u>.

After entering all the values, the row appears. Similarly, you can enter more values in other cells. Now you can see on your screen that data in the column named Salary Drawn On is marked as ####. We have entered the data in correct format but due to width of the cell, which is very small, the data present in the cell is not looking properly. To view data in the proper format, you have to adjust the cell size, which we will discuss later in this chapter. In next section, you learn about different ways to select a cell.

Using Different Ways to Select Cells

In Microsoft Excel, selecting cells refers to selecting text, number, or alphanumeric value present in a cell. Without selecting cells, you cannot perform any calculations in Excel. For example, if you want to find the sum of values appearing in three cells, first you have to select corresponding cell and then perform the calculation. In Excel, you can select a cell directly in the document window or from a cell address. After selecting a cell, you can cut or copy the cell and then paste the cell within the same sheet or any other sheet. Selected cells have bold outlining in the worksheet. To select a single cell, place the mouse pointer on the cell and click it. For multiple cell selection, click the left mouse button and drag until the cells you want to select are outlined.

Continuous Selection

When you select more than one cell without leaving any single cell between them, then it is called continuous selection. To make a continuous selection, you have to click a cell, hold shift button and then click the cell till where you want to make the selection. As the result, the selected cells will look outlined.

Non-Continuous Selection

If the cells are selected randomly from the worksheet; it is called non-continuous selection. While making non-continuous selection, either select random cells vertically within a column or select cells horizontally across different columns within a single common row. You cannot select cells randomly across different columns. For example, you cannot select A1 and B9 cells together. However, you can vertically select A1 and A4 cells or horizontally select A5 and C5 cells.

It means if you will select different rows from worksheet, then columns must be same. Or when you will select different columns from worksheet, then rows must be same. To make a non-continuous selection, just hold the Ctrl key and click the cells, which you wan to select.

If you do not follow the rule given for non-continuous selection, then after selecting the data when you click the Copy or Cut button, then an error message appears on the Excel worksheet. Both the ways of selection have their own advantage, if you want to select the whole sheet or a big region on the sheet, then continuous selection is useful. On the other hand, if you wan to select the random cells or data from different locations on a worksheet, then non-continuous selection is used.

Using Cut, Copy, and Paste Commands

The cut, copy, and paste commands allow you to easily move data from one application to another or from one location to another. These commands are common to all the application software. All these commands are present in the Home tab of Microsoft Excel. You are required to select some data to work with these commands because if you do not have any data selected, then these commands will not work in Excel. Now, select some data from the worksheet, and let us first learn to work with the Cut command.

The Cut Command

The Cut command is useful when you want to move the original data from its current location. After selecting some data, perform the following steps:

1. Click the **Home** tab at the top of the Excel window.

2. Click the **Cut** button in Clipboard group which is just below the Home tab. As the result, the selected data gets dotted outline which means the data is ready to move to the new location.

The Paste Command

The Paste command is useful when you want to paste the data, which you have cut from the original location. Following are the steps to paste the copied data on the selected location:

1. Click the **Home** tab at the top of the window.

2. Click the **Paste** button in Clipboard group. The cut data will move to the selected location. These commands can be used on both continuous as well as non-continuous selections.

The Copy Command

The Copy command does not move the selected data from its original location, rather creates its duplicate copy to be pasted to the next location. Perform these steps to copy the selected data:

1. Click the **Home** tab at the top of the window.

2. Click the **Copy** button in Clipboard group. The selected region gets dotted outline, which means the data is ready to move to the new location.

3. Click the **Paste** button in Clipboard group. The copied data will move to the selected location.

Performing Spelling-Check in Worksheet

Spell-checker compares the words typed by you to a dictionary of words present in an application and suggests corrections for wrongly spelled words. However, the spell-checker cannot detect the wrong usage of a correctly spelled word. A spell-checker operates at the word level. If there is any error in spelling of a word, then it gives a list of words similar to the incorrect word. You can select any one of them to correct the word. Spell-checkers operate at user's request for checking an entire document or worksheet at once.

Spell-checking operation can be performed in two ways on a worksheet – on the selected area and on the entire sheet. When you perform spell-checking on a selected area, it checks the spell errors only on the selected region. Whereas, when you perform spell-check on the entire sheet, it checks the whole sheet for spelling errors. Perform the following steps after selecting the data:

1. Click the **Review** tab at the top of the Excel window.

2. Click the **Spelling** button under the <u>Proofing</u> group.

The Spelling English (United States) dialog box appears. There are various buttons on the right-side of the dialog box. With these buttons, you can ignore misspelled words or replace them with the correct one. If there is a word (like name of a person, state, or street) which is appearing as misspelled word but you want to retain it, then use the Add to Dictionary button and include that name in the dictionary. Next time, MS Excel will not consider that word as misspelled.

Using Auto Correct

Excel 2013 provides auto correct feature, which checks the errors made by the user while entering data. This feature can operate automatically or on user's request. This feature is present in the Spelling English (United States) dialog box. If you click the AutoCorrect button in the Spelling dialog box, it corrects the wrongly spelled words automatically. The drawback of the auto correct feature is that it replaces the wrong word with the first word present in the Suggestion list; therefore it is not used frequently.

Formatting Cells

Formatting cells describe how data will be represented in cells after completing the task on the worksheet. With formatting cells, we can change the appearance of the cell without changing its value. In this way, a user can easily differentiate the data by formatting the cells. You can present the output in a better way, by using various formatting styles. You can also customize the worksheet to make it easier to read. In this section, we discuss different ways to change the cell size, font, color, and orientation.

Adjusting Row and Column Area

Excel automatically adjusts the cell size but sometimes, a user can also adjust the cell size according to the requirement. There are two ways to change the size of a cell – manual and automatic. In manual method the size of a cell is changed manually, and in automatic method the size of the cell is changed automatically.

Adjust Row Height Automatically

The height of a row changes when the size of font is changed. Before setting the cell size, first select the cells, for which you want to adjust the size. After selecting the data, perform the following steps to set the row height:

1. Click the **Home** tab at the top of the Excel window.

2. Click the **Format** button under the <u>Cells</u> group. It opens a dropdown list.

3. Click the **AutoFit Row Height** option from the dropdown list. As the result, Excel will automatically set the row height depending on the data present in the cell.

Adjust Column Width Automatically

To set the size of Column Width automatically, you need to click the **AutoFit Column Width** option present in the <u>Format</u> dropdown list. After applying both the options, that is AutoFit Row Height and AutoFit Column Width, size of the row and column are changed. You will see on your screen that the cell size is adjusted according to the data present in the selected list.

Specify Row Height

In Excel, you can also change the appearance of cells by adjusting the height of rows according to the specified value. Increasing the row height adds extra space between rows and makes the worksheet look specious. Perform the following steps to change row height:

1. Click the **Home** tab, and click the **Format** button under the <u>Cells</u> group.

2. Click the **Row Height** option from the dropdown list. A Row Height dialog box appears with default value.

3. **Type** a new value to change the height of rows. In our case, we type: **20**.

4. Click the **OK** button to apply the changes. As the result, the height of selected row is changed. This way, you can increase or decrease the height of rows.

Specify Column Width

Sometimes, data consists of lengthy words and needs more space. In such case, you can change the width of column as per the data. Perform the following steps to change the column width as per requirement:

1. Click the **Home** tab, and click the **Format** button in the Cells group.

2. Click the **Column Width** option in the dropdown list to open its dialog box on the screen. The default Column Width, 8.43, appears in the dialog box.

3. **Type** your desired value beside the Column Width option. In our case, we type: **15**.

4. Click the **OK** button to apply the changes. As the result, the width of the selected column is changed on the worksheet. You will see on your screen that the cell size is adjusted according to the specified column width.

Setting Currency Symbol, Decimal Places, Date, and Time

When you enter some value in a cell, MS Excel handles the value according to the type of formatting you have applied to the cell. In this section, you learn about various settings of a cell and how to change their setting.

Currency Symbol

Currency symbol is used to add different symbols for different currencies according to the requirement. Perform the following steps to add currency symbol:

1. **Select** the column in which you want to add Currency symbol. In our case, we select entire <u>Salary</u> column.

2. Click the **Home** tab, and click the **Dialog Box Launcher** button in the <u>Number</u> group, as shown in picture 2.6.

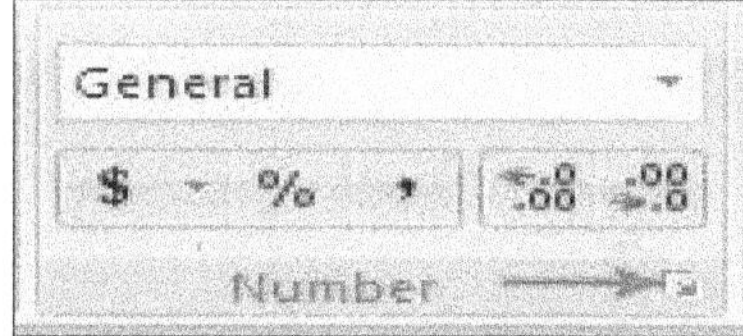

Picture 2.6

3. It opens the <u>Format Cells</u> dialog box, as shown in picture 2.7. Now click the **Currency** category on the left side in the dialog box.

4. **Click** the down arrow button beside the **Symbol** option on the right side in the dialog box.

5. Click the **Rs. English (India)** currency format from the dropdown list.

6. Click the **OK** button in the dialog box to apply the changes.

The Format Cells dialog box disappears. As the result, the selected cells appear with chosen currency format. In the next section, we will learn about decimal places.

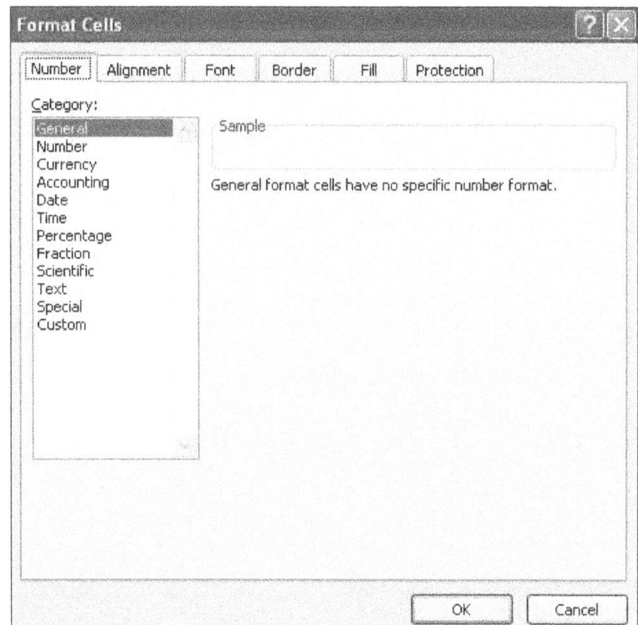

Picture 2.7

Decimal Places

To set decimal places on a cell, first select any cell. In the given example, we have selected the same data which we had selected in the previous section. Now perform the following steps to set decimal places on the Salary column:

1. Click the **Home** tab, and click the **Dialog Box Launcher** button in the <u>Number</u> group. It opens the **Format Cells** dialog box on the screen.

2. Click the **Currency** category on the left side in the dialog box.

3. **Type** a number in the spin box beside the <u>Decimal places</u> option.

The number typed reflects how much digits should appear after decimal symbol in a number. In our case, we type: **2** to display two digits in a number after the decimal symbol. The maximum value for decimal place is 30. You can set the value for decimal place within this limit.

4. Click the **OK** button to apply the changes.

As the result, in the Salary column (E), the width of the data is increased but the width of the column is still same. That is way the data present in it will not look clear on your screen. Now to show the data properly, you have to change the width of column. Perform the following steps to change the width of the column:

1. Click the **Home** tab, and click the **Format** button in <u>Cells</u> group.

2. Click the **Column Width** option from the dropdown list. It opens the Column Width dialog box.

3. **Type** the suitable value beside the Column Width option to increase the column width in order to display the hidden data.

4. Click the **OK** button to apply the new width to the column. As the result, the selected column (E) appears with increased width and the data starts appearing properly.

Setting Date

At the time of entering data, user might the date in his own format or the user might enter month number ahead of day number, by mistake. In such a situation, using a common date format in the worksheet is an ideal option. Excel provides different date formats, which are used to represent date. Perform the following steps to set the date format in selected cells:

1. Click the **Home** tab, and click the **Format** button in the Cells group.

2. Click the **Format Cells** option from the dropdown list. It opens the Format Cells dialog box.

3. Click the **Date** category on the left side. Then under <u>Type</u> option, **click** the desired date format.

4. **Click** the down arrow button under the **Locale (location)** option. It opens a dropdown list.

5. **Select** the desired language in the dropdown list that you want to use for displaying date. In our case, we select the **Faroese** option. This option will display the date in the format of English language spoken and used in India.

6. Click the **OK** button to apply the date format to selected cells.

In your worksheet, the Column D (Leave) is set to new date format but due to the small size of column-width, dates may not appear properly. In such a situation, broadening the column width is suitable option. To do so, open the Column Width dialog box, type suitable value, and press the Enter key. You have already done it once in the previous section of this lesson.

Setting Time
To set time in a cell, you need to select a column or row in which you want to set Time format. In our case, we are setting time format on Salary Drawn on column. Perform these steps to set Time format:

1. Click the **Home** tab, and click the **Format** button in the Cells group.

2. Click the **Format Cells** option from the dropdown list. It opens the Format Cells dialog box.

3. Click the **Time** category on the left side. Then **click** the desired time format under <u>Type</u> list box.

By default, the language and country selected at the time of applying Date format should appear under Locale (location). Ideally, date and time format should appear in same language. In case some other language and country is appearing under Locale (location) option, then click the down-arrow button under the **Locale (location)** option and select **Faroese** option in the dropdown list.

4. Click the **OK** button to apply time format to the selected cells. As the result, the selected cells in the worksheet appear with new time format.

Lesson 3
Working with Font and Highlighting Cells
Excel provides a various aspect related to font. In Excel, you can change the font, its style and size according to your requirement. You can also highlight the data for attention to the viewer. Let's start with changing the font size.

Changing Font
Whenever you enter data (word, number or character) in a worksheet, it is displayed with default font setting of the Microsoft Excel program. However at any time, you can change the font to make data attractive. To do so, first you need to make decision in which part of worksheet you want to change the font – cell, row or columns. In the example given below, we select the data in the worksheet, and then perform the following steps:

1. Click the **Home** tab, and click the **Dialog Box Launcher** button under the <u>Font</u> group, as shown in picture 2.8. It opens the <u>Format Cells</u> dialog box with **Font** tab selected.

2. **Click** the font name under the <u>Font</u> tab. In our case, we click **Pristina** font name.

3. Click the **OK** button to apply the change to the font of selected cells.

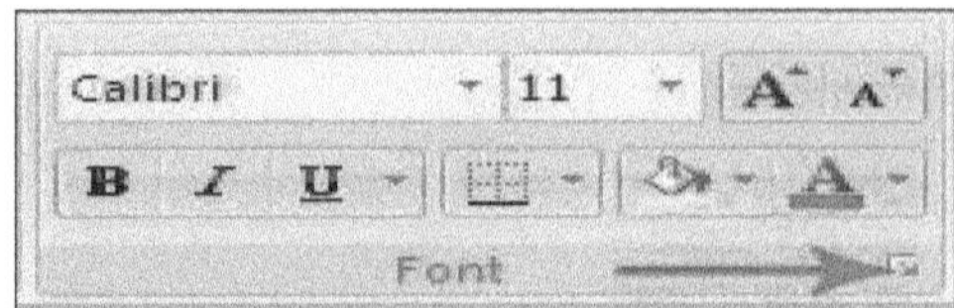

Picture 2.8

Changing Font Style

There are mainly four types of font styles – Regular, Italic, Bold, and Bold Italic. You can change font style of the data depending on your choice. Let's now perform the following steps and learn to change the font style:

1. **Select** the data from the cell, and click the **Home** tab at the top.

2. Click the **Dialog Box Launcher** button under the Font group.

3. Click the **Bold Italic** style under the Font tab. As the result, the font of selected cells will tilt towards right-side and the tilted font of selected cells grows and appears emphasized than the data of remaining cells in the worksheet.

4. Click the **OK** button at the bottom of the dialog box.

You can also change the font style from the Format Cells dialog box. To do so, click the Dialog Box Launcher button in the Font group of Home tab and click a style listed under the Font style option of Font tab.

Changing the Font Size

You can specify the importance of data by changing the size of font in a worksheet. For example, you can increase the font size of leading text in the worksheet in order to make it as heading for the worksheet. Besides creating headings, you can increase font size of some cell's values in order to make them stand apart in the worksheet. Let's perform the following steps and learn to change the font size:

1. **Select** the data from cell A3 to E7 in your worksheet.

2. Click the **Dialog Launcher** button in the Font group of Home tab.

3. **Click** the desired font size under the Font tab. In our case, we select Font size as **14**.

4. Click the **OK** button to close the dialog box. As the result, the size of the font in the selected cell increases.

Highlighting Cells Using Fill Color

Highlighting the data is used to gain the attention of a viewer. In MS Excel, you can highlight data by changing the background color of its cell. Let's now perform the following steps to fill the color in cells and change the background:

1. **Select** the data from cell A3 to E7 in your worksheet.

2. Click the **Dialog Launcher** button in the Font group of Home tab. It opens the Format Cells dialog box.

3. Click the **Fill** tab in the dialog box, and **choose** the desired color under the Background Color option.

4. Click the **OK** button to apply the color in the background of the selected cells. As the result, the selected cells appear with new background color in worksheet.

This is the first way to highlight the cell. There is another way to highlight the cell known as cell styles, which we discuss in the upcoming section.

Highlighting Cells Using Cell Styles

Applying Cell Styles is the second way to highlight cells. In this method, by-default, many styles are present in the list. This is very different from the previous method of highlighting cells. In this method, there are more benefits, such as when you move your mouse pointer to any one of the style present in the list, then you can see the effect on the sheet without applying the style. Just move the mouse-pointer over the Cell Style and see preview on the worksheet. When you want to give effects on the worksheet, cell styles is very useful, as it helps you to give different looks to your worksheet. Let's perform the following steps and learn to apply cell styles to a selected range:

1. **Select** some data in the worksheet. In our case, we select data from cell A8 to E14.

2. Click the **Home** tab, and click the **Cell Styles** button under the Styles group. It opens a dropdown list in which various styles are available.

3. **Click** the desired cell style from the dropdown list. In our case, we click the **Note** cell style. The selected range in the worksheet appears in Note style and the background of the selected range turns yellowish.

Setting Cell Alignment

Before discussing about cell alignment, it is necessary for you to know what cell alignment is. Alignment means changing the position of data within the cell. In MS Excel, there are two default ways to align the data within a cell – Vertically and Horizontally. At any given time, you can use Vertical and Horizontal alignments together. If you are not satisfied with the default alignments, you can go for the Custom Orientation to position the data at different angles within a cell as per your requirement. Excel also provides a feature in which you can merge and centre the text across several cells. Let's start with vertical cell alignment.

Vertical Cell Alignment

Vertical cell alignment is used to position the data in top, middle, or at bottom directions within a cell. The default Vertical alignment in a worksheet is Bottom. To change the vertical alignment in a cell, select some data and click the Vertical alignment button in the top row of Alignment group of Home tab. Let's now perform the following steps to change the vertical alignment of a cell:

1. **Select** some cells in the worksheet. In our case, we select data from cell B8 to C12.

2. Click the **Home** tab, and click the **Top Align** button under the <u>Alignment</u> group. As the result, the new alignment applies to the selected cells and the data in the selected cells moves in the top direction.

Horizontal Cell Alignment

Horizontal cell alignment is used to set the data in left, center, or right direction within a cell. The default Horizontal alignment in a worksheet is Left. To change the Horizontal alignment in a cell, select some data and click the Horizontal alignment button in the second row of the Alignment group of Home tab. Let's perform the following steps and learn to change the Horizontal alignment:

1. **Select** some cells in the worksheet. In our case, we select data from cell B8 to C12.

2. Click the **Home** tab, and click the **Center Align** button under the <u>Alignment</u> group. The new Horizontal alignment applies to selected cells and the data within the selected cells appears in Center direction.

Merge and Center

Using the Merge and Center command, you can merge more than one cell into a larger cell and align the data center. You can use the Merge and Center command to join cells spread across columns or rows. This command is useful in preparing columnar or row labels. Let's now perform the following steps and learn to use the Merge and Center command:

1. **Select** cells on which you want to apply the Merge and Center command. For this command, generally those cells are selected which contain data that must span across different columns and act as label for rest of the data. In our case, we select cells **A3 to E7**.

2. Click the **Home** tab, and click the **Merge & Center** button under the <u>Alignment</u> group. If you click the down-arrow button beside the Merge & Center button, a dropdown list appears. Using options available in the dropdown list, you can Merge and Unmerge a cell.

Setting the Orientation of a Cell

Orientation means to rotate the data of a cell at an angle either in clockwise or anti-clockwise direction. This command is used to emphasize the data in the cell. Let's now perform the following steps to change the orientation of data present in a cell:

1. **Select** the cell to which you want to apply the Orientation. In our case, we select cell B2.

2. Click the **Home** tab, and then click the **Dialog Box Launcher** button under the <u>Alignment</u> group, as shown in picture 2.9.

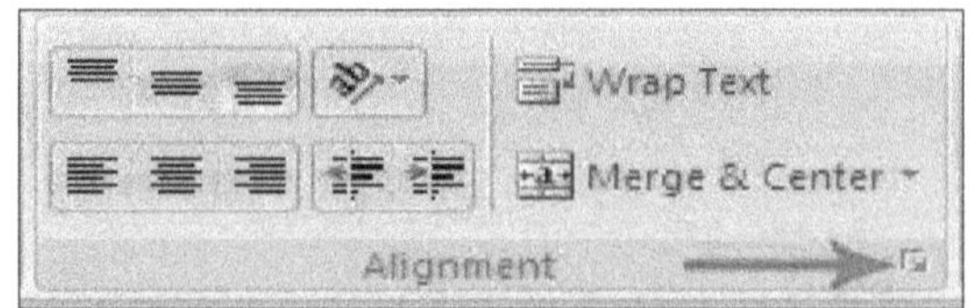

Picture 2.9

It opens the **Format Cells** dialog box. By default, the <u>Alignment</u> tab will appear first. In case, it is not appearing, then click it.

3. **Set** the value of angle by dragging <u>Text hand</u> icon under the <u>Orientation</u> section, as shown in picture 3.0 with the red arrow. You can also change the value of degree manually by typing the value in the spin box beside the Degree option.

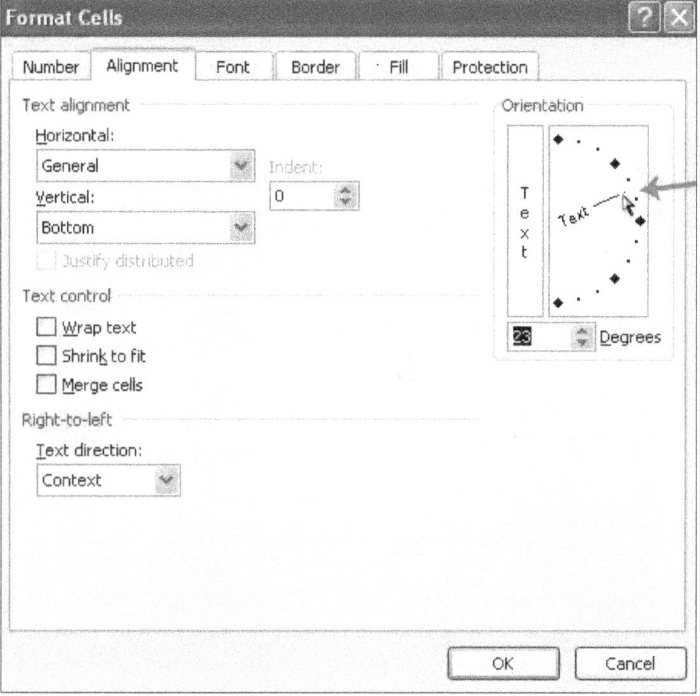

Picture 3.0

4. Click the **OK** button to apply the orientation. As the result, the text present in the selected cell is set angular.

Setting the Format and Other Properties of a Worksheet

In the previous section, we have discussed about formatting cells, in this section we will discuss about formatting worksheets. In formatting cells, we made changes only on cells while in formatting worksheets; we will make changes on the entire worksheet. In this section, you learn to format a worksheet by applying margins, inserting and customizing headers and footers, applying a background, renaming a worksheet, and selecting the center page alignment. Let's begin with setting margins to a worksheet.

Applying Margins to a Worksheet

Margins are set to define the print area of a worksheet. Sometimes, when you print the data present on the worksheet, due to improper margin setting some part of the data gets lapse during printing. In such case, it becomes necessary to set margins properly. There are six parts of margin – Top, Bottom, Left, Right, Header, and Footer. By default, three margin settings are given in the list, first is Normal setting, second is Wide setting, and third is Narrow setting. A user can also set margins by using Custom Margins option. The Custom Margin option is used to set the margin settings manually. You can choose any one of these settings to set margins in your worksheet. Perform the following steps to set margins in worksheet:

1. Click the **Page Layout** tab at the top of the Excel window.

2. Click the **Margins** button under <u>Page Setup</u> group. It opens the **Margin** dropdown list.

3. **Click** the desired page layout from the dropdown list. By default, the presently applied page setup appears highlighted in the list.

In Excel, you can also use Custom Margin option to set the margin settings manually. If you want to use Custom Martin option, you can perform the following steps:

1. In the <u>Margin</u> dropdown list, click the **Custom Margin** option at the bottom.

It opens the **Page Setup** dialog box with <u>Margins</u> tab appearing in front with six margins **Top**, **Header**, **Left**, **Right**, **Bottom**, and **Footer**.

2. Type **1** under <u>Left</u>. Then type **1.25** under <u>Right</u>.

3. Click the **OK** button to apply new left and right margins.

Inserting Header and Footer

You often need to include some information about your document at the top (the Header) or at the bottom (the Footer) of each printed sheet. Headers and footers are those little identifiers that run through the top and bottom of your document, providing important background information about it. They can include page numbering, title, author name, chapter number, and date. Perform the following steps to insert header and footer in a worksheet:

1. **Click** a cell in the worksheet, and click the **Insert** tab at the top of the Excel window.

2. Click the **Headers & Footer** button under the <u>Text</u> group.

An editable region appears on top of the worksheet. This editable region is known as Header where you can add text as quick reference about the worksheet. Excel shows three regions in Header, Left, Center, and Right. Also, the horizontal and vertical rulers appear on the worksheet. These rulers help you to increase or decrease the size of header regions. You can add content in any of the three regions. It is as easy as typing and formatting.

3. **Type** page header in any region of the header.

At the time of including headers or footers, you must have observed the appearance of additional Design tab under the Header & Footer Tools contextual menu. This tab contains all the tools that we can use when working with the Headers and Footers option in MS Excel. You can also pick the predefined Headers and Footers option from galleries. You can navigate between headers and footers and insert page numbers & dates.

Like header, the footer also contains three regions – Left, Center, and Right. You can add the required information in any of the three regions, as and when required.

Customizing Header and Footer

In Excel, some new functionality has been added to the Headers and Footers option. Here is the detail of those functionalities:

- **Color:** Provides colored formatting.
- **Different first page:** Allows users to specify a unique header and footer for the first page. This is very useful for reports with title pages or table of contents where header or footer might need to be different.
- **Different Odd and Even Pages:** Allows users to specify unique header and footer for odd and even pages.
- **Align with Page Margins:** Allows users to choose their header and footer margins to the page margin.
- **Scale with the Document:** Allows headers and footers to ignore the page scaling set for a given sheet.

Applying a Background

Microsoft Excel allows you to set the background image on your worksheet, to make it effective. Sometimes it seems that the worksheet on which you are presenting your report need some background image to look effective. This command changes the entire background of a worksheet. Perform the following steps to set an image on your worksheet:

1. **Click** any cell in the worksheet, and click the **Page Layout** tab at the top.

2. Click the **Background** button under the Page Setup group. It opens the **Insert Picture** dialog box.

3. **Select** the location where images are located using Look in: combo box. Then **select** the desired picture and click the **Insert** button at the bottom of the dialog box.

Renaming a Worksheet

Sometimes you may want to rename a worksheet due to some reason. At the bottom of each worksheet in Excel's window, a small tab indicates the name of the worksheet in the workbook. Excel names these worksheets using a default name. These names (Sheet1, Sheet2, Sheet3, and so on) are not very descriptive. You might want to rename your worksheet to reflect what they contain. Perform the following steps to rename a worksheet:

1. **Open** a worksheet that you want to rename. In our case, we will rename the same worksheet.

2. Click the **Home** tab, and click the **Format** button under the Cells group.

3. Click the **Rename Sheet** option from the dropdown list. The name of the worksheet in the Sheets tab gets highlighted.

Now, you can rename the sheet by just typing the name for the sheet. In our case, we type **Salary** to rename the worksheet. You can see on your screen that Sheet1 is changed to Salary. In the next section, let's learn to color the Sheet tab.

Adding a Worksheet

While working on a worksheet, you require more worksheets on the same workbook. Perform the following steps to insert new worksheets in your workbook:

1. Click the **Home** tab, and click the **Insert** button under Cells group.

2. Click the **Insert Sheet** option from the dropdown list. As the result, a new worksheet is included in the workbook.

Selecting the Center Page Alignment

Center page alignment is used to set working area at the center of the page. There are two ways to set the Center alignment of the page – Horizontally and Vertically. The Horizontal alignment sets the working area to the center of the page horizontally while Vertical alignment sets the working area to the center of the page vertically. Let's perform the following steps to learn to set the Center page alignment:

1. Click the **Page Layout** tab at the top, and click the **Margins** button under the Page Setup group.

2. Click the **Custom Margins** option from the dropdown list. It opens the Page Setup dialog box, as shown in picture 3.1.

3. Select the **Vertically** checkbox under the Center on page section, as shown in picture with the red arrow.

4. Click the **OK** button to apply new Center page alignment.

If required, you can select both the Horizontally and Vertically checkboxes. Selecting both checkboxes center aligns the data from all margins of a page. Now, let's learn to save a workbook.

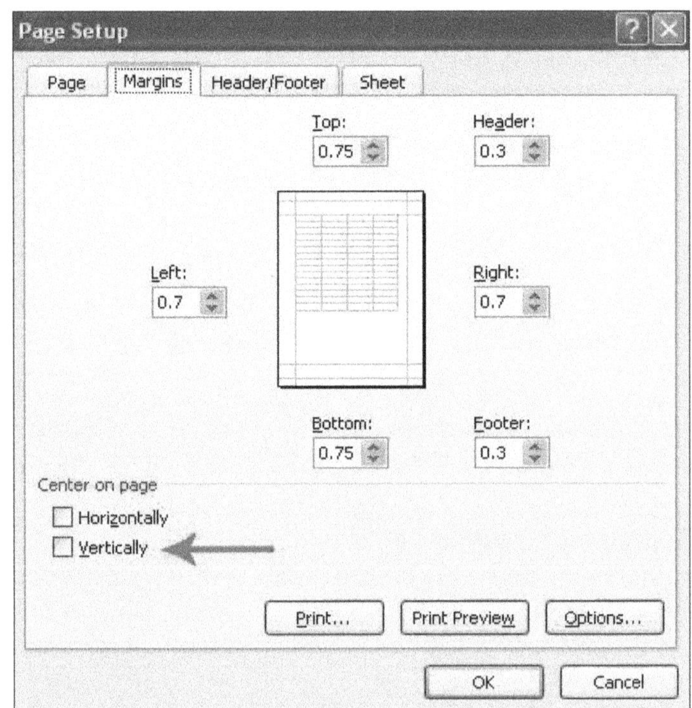

Picture 3.1

Saving Workbook

Saving workbook is an essential part of Excel, because if the work done in the worksheet is not saved, you cannot use that data again in the future. To make it usable for future, it is necessary to save the data. When you close a worksheet after making changes on it, Microsoft Excel prompts you to save the document. Perform the following steps to save a workbook:

1. Click the **Office** button, and click the **Save** option from the dropdown list. It opens the Save As dialog box on the screen.

2. **Type** the name of workbook beside the File name option.

3. **Select** a location where you want to save the file in the Navigation pane.

4. Click the **Save** button at the bottom of the dialog box. As the result, the workbook is saved in your computer.

Assign Password to Worksheet

Password is assigned to a worksheet to protect the sheet from the unauthorized users. Sometimes confidential data of the worksheet needs to be protected so that no one can access the worksheet. In such cases, password is assigned to the worksheet. Here are the steps to set the password to a worksheet:

1. Click the **Review** tab at the top, and click the **Protect Sheet** button under the Changes group.

2. **Type** the password under the Password to unprotect sheet textbox.

3. Click the **OK** button which opens a Confirm Password dialog box.

4. **Retype** the password under the Reenter password to proceed textbox.

5. Click the **OK** button. Now the worksheet is protected from the unauthorized users. If you double-click the worksheet to edit, you have to unprotect the worksheet, which is discussed in the next section.

Unprotect a Worksheet

To make changes in a worksheet, you have to unprotect the sheet, if it is protected. The Unprotect option is present in the Changes group. Perform the following steps to unprotect a worksheet:

1. Click the **Review** tab, and click the **Unprotect Sheet** button under the Changes group.

2. **Type** the password beside the Password textbox. This password must be same as that of entered during protecting worksheet.

3. Click the **OK** button in the dialog box. Now the worksheet is unprotected.

Preparing Worksheet for Printing

Once the work on the worksheet is completed, you can change the setting of the worksheet, such as print title, print gridlines, and row and column headings; for better printing.

Adding Print Titles, Row and Column Headings, and Gridlines for Printing

In the Adding printing title, we select the area of the worksheet that we want to print. In this process, you can set the rows and columns that you want to print. The Row and Column heading checkboxes allow you to show indexes of rows and columns on the printed document and the Gridline checkbox allows you to show the gridline on the printed document. The steps to add print titles to a worksheet:

1. Click the **Page Layout** tab, and click the **Print Titles** button under the Page Setup group.

2. Click the **Collapse Dialog** button beside the Print area option. The Page Setup dialog box squeezes.

In worksheet, define the print area by selecting cells. The range of selected cells appears in the Page Setup dialog box.

3. Click the **Expand Dialog** button after selecting print area. The Page Setup dialog box reappears.

4. Click the **Collapse Dialog** button beside the Rows to repeat at top option in the Page Setup dialog box.

A **Page Setup – Rows to repeat at top** dialog box appears on the worksheet. Highlight the row that you want to repeat at the top of each printed page.

5. Click the **Expand Dialog** button which makes the Page Setup dialog box reappear.

6. Click the **Collapse Dialog** button beside the Columns to repeat at left option. The **Page Setup – Columns to repeat at left** dialog box appears on the worksheet.

7. **Select** the column that you want to repeat at the left of each printed page.

8. Click the **Expand Dialog** button which makes the Page Setup dialog box reappear.

9. Select the **Gridlines** and **Row and column headings** checkboxes under the Print checkbox.

10. Click the **Print Preview** button to see the preview of the worksheet. The output of the page appears on the screen.

Inserting Breaks
The Breaks option is available in Excel to insert break in print area. Suppose, there are thousands of records in a worksheet and it is not possible to print them on a single sheet. Inserting break on the worksheet allows the data between break points to be printed on a separate sheet. Perform the following steps to insert break on a sheet:

1. **Click** a cell where you want to insert Break.

2. Click the **Page Layout** tab, and click the **Breaks** button in the Page Setup group.

3. Click the **Insert Page Break** present in the dropdown list.

As the result, a break is inserted where you have selected the cell. In our case, we have selected the ninth row, so there is a break inserted after the eighth row. This way, you can insert Break whenever you want to differentiate the data.

Viewing the Print Preview of a Worksheet
Before printing, it is necessary to see Print Preview because in this option, you can see how the printed output will come. We have already discussed print preview in the Adding Print Titles section, but there

we have given a print preview just to view the output of the document to be printed. However, now we discuss about print preview in detail. Perform the following steps to see Print Preview:

1. Click **Office** button to open a dropdown list.

2. Select the **Print** submenu and click the **Print Preview** option.

Microsoft Excel displays the preview of worksheet. You can see the preview of the document when you are setting the print option; this helps you to modify your worksheet if required.

Printing a Worksheet

You can print the worksheet after making appropriate changes. Perform the following steps to print a worksheet:

1. Click **Office** button to open a dropdown list.

2. Select the **Print** submenu and click the **Print** option.

The **Print** dialog box appears. The <u>Name</u> option displays the name of default printer. Under Print range, option to print all pages in a worksheet appears selected.

3. Click the **Page(s)** radio button under the <u>Print range</u> option.

4. **Type** page number beside the <u>From</u> option to specify the starting page number from where you want to begin the printing.

5. **Type** page number beside the <u>To</u> option in order to specify the page number up to which you want to print the document. We have set the Print range from 5 to 15. It means if there are 20 pages in the workbook, then only pages from 5 to 15 will be printed and rest of the pages will not be printed.

6. Click the **OK** button at the bottom of the dialog box.

Lesson 4
Conditional Formatting, Sorting, and Filtering Data
Conditional formatting is a very popular tool used in Excel to format data. It can be used to visually annotate the data for analytical and presentation purposes. In Excel 2013, this feature has been improved and additional several new visualizations, such as a new user interface (UI) for adding, removing and managing conditional formats; several conditional formatting rules; and the facility to use more than three conditions. You can arrange data quickly by using the sort and filter features. The sort feature in Excel is now enhanced and can be used to sort the data by color. In addition, the AutoFilter feature in Excel can be used to simplify the filtering process.

In this chapter, you learn to apply various types of conditional formatting that includes top/bottom rules, data bars, and Icon sets. In addition, you learn to modify rules in conditional formatting. You also learn about sorting data and finally applying filter on data.

About Conditional Formatting

Conditional formatting is a tool that allows a user to apply different formats to a cell or a range of cells. The formatting of a cell changes according to the content of the cell or the value of the formula. As it is clear from the name, the formatting changes are applied when certain conditions are fulfilled. You can apply conditional formatting to a cell to make it look different form other cells. For example, you can set a cell appear italic only when the value of a cell is greater than 50 and appear green when the value of a cell is greater than 100. Once the value of the cell meets the condition defined in the format, the setting you choose gets applied to the cell or a range of cells.

The Conditional Formatting tool is improved in Microsoft Excel 2013, and it allows you to visualize the numeric data. It allows you to apply cell formatting selectively and automatically, depending on the content of the cells. Conditional Formatting is a useful way to quickly indentify wrong cell entries or cells of a particular type. You can use a format to make particular cells easy to indentify. An example of Conditional Formatting is shown in picture 3.2.

	A	B	C	D	E	F
1			Result			
2	Name	Science	Maths	Liter.	Total	
3	Pradeep	78	92	79	249	
4	Satish	76	79	80	235	
5	Yogesh	69	82	69	220	
6	Dhanesh	66	76	78	220	
7	Jagdeep	80	69	80	229	
8	Prabhat	83	86	72	241	
9						
10						

Picture 3.2

In picture 3.2, a worksheet is shown where you can see the marks of various students of a class in different subjects. In the preceding example, if the total marks of a student are greater than 220, then the cell is highlighted with the green check mark, otherwise the cell is highlighted with the red cross mark. Now we will discuss how to apply different types of conditional formatting and modify the rules of conditional formatting. But before that, let's learn about merging cells.

Merging Cells

In picture 3.2, you can see that from the cell A1 to E1, all the five cells are merged and has become one cell. When you merge cells, it helps you to place the text in the middle or anywhere you want. Perform the following steps to merge cells:

1. Select the cells from **A1 to E1** by dragging the mouse-pointer over them.

2. Click the dropdown button of **Merge & Center** in the <u>Alignment</u> group of the Home tab.

3. Select the **Merge Cells** option. As the result, all the five cells are merged in the worksheet.

Applying Conditional Formatting

There are different types of options in the Conditional Formatting tool in Excel 2013, such as Highlight Cell Rules, Top/Bottom Rules, Data Bars, Color Scales, and Icon Sets. To apply conditional formatting, there must be some data present on the spreadsheet. Therefore, let's perform the following steps to enter some data in a worksheet:

1. **Click** the cell A1 and type **Sales Wise Analysis**.
2. Set text to the center using **Merge & Center** option present in the Alignment group of the Home tab.
3. Click the cell **A2** and type **Branch Name**.

4. Click the cell **B2** and type **Q1 Sales**.
5. Click the cell **C2** and type **Q2 Sales**.
6. Click the cell **D2** and type **Q3 Sales**.
7. Click the cell **E2** and type **Q4 Sales**.
8. Click the cell **A3** and type **Delhi**.
9. Click the cell **B3** and type **Q1 Sales**.

10. Similarly, type values in **C3**, **D3**, and **E3** cells.
11. **Enter** some more values in the cells below the column headings.

After entering the data in the worksheet, now you can apply conditional formatting on the data. In this section, we are going to discuss three types of conditional formatting: Top/Bottom Rules, Data Bars, and Icon Sets.

Top/Bottom Rules of Conditional Formatting

The Top/Bottom Rules conditional formatting is used to highlight top or bottom values in a range. By default, Microsoft Excel displays ten top or bottom values but you can change this count by increasing or decreasing the number. The different options present in Top 10 Rules are as follows:

- **Top 10 Items:** Displays top 10 values present in the selected cells. However, it never means that only top 10 items will be shown as highlighted items present in the list, you can set this value according to your requirement.
- **Top 10%:** Returns top 10% values present in the selected range.
- **Bottom 10 Items:** Displays minimum values from the given list. In other words, you can say it gives the lowest 10 items present in a list.
- **Bottom 10%:** Displays bottom 10% values in the selected region.
- **Above Average:** Highlights all the values above the average value of the selected list.
- **Below Average:** Highlights all the values below the average value.

Let's now undertake the following steps and learn to apply the Top/Bottom Rules of condition formatting:

1. **Select** some numerical data in the worksheet that you entered in the previous section.

2. Click the **Home** tab, and click the **Conditional Formatting** button under the <u>Styles</u> group. It opens a dropdown list with different categories of conditional formatting.

3. Select the **Top/Bottom Rules** option under the Conditional Formatting dropdown list.

4. Click the **Top 10 Items** option in the submenu. The Top 10 Items dialog box appears on the screen.

By default, the dialog box displays 10 in order to display top ten values in the range but you can change number and highlight consequent number of top values in the range.

5. Click the **Format cells that rank in the TOP** list box to select a color for highlighting top values in the range.

6. Click **OK** in the dialog box. As the result, the worksheet appears with top ten highlighted values.

7. **Click** anywhere in the worksheet to remove the highlight. After learning about the Top/Bottom conditional formatting, let's learn about Data Bars conditional formatting.

Data Bars Conditional Formatting
In this type of conditional formatting, horizontal color bars appear beside each value in the cell range. Data bars are another way to apply conditional formatting on a cell range. This formatting is used when you want to show bars in a cell range along with values. Data bars give you an opportunity to create visual effects on the data, which helps you to see how the value of a cell is compared with other cells. Data bars give you facility to quickly understand large quantity of information. Data bars make it easier to compare the value of a cell relative to all other selected cells. Suppose you have a large amount of data on a worksheet, and you want to differentiate the largest and smallest value; in this case, data bars are very useful. Perform the following steps to learn to apply the Data Bars conditional formatting:

1. **Select** some numerical data in the worksheet.

2. Click the **Home** tab, and click the **Conditional Formatting** button under the <u>Styles</u> group.

3. Select the **Data Bars** category from the Conditional Formatting dropdown list.

4. **Click** the desired color scheme for data bars from the Data Bars submenu. As the result, the data bars appear in each cell depicting its value.

5. **Click** anywhere in the sheet to remove the highlight from the cell range.

If you look at your screen, you can easily indentify the largest as well as the smallest values in the list. Excel is comparing the values in each of the selected cells and drawing data bar in each cell representing the value of that cell related to other cells present in the selected range. The bar makes it easy for users to pick out the largest and smallest values in the range.

When you click the More Rules option in the Data Bar menu, a New Formatting Rule dialog box appears, which is divided into two sections – Select a Rule Type and Edit the Rule Description. You can change the Rule Type present in the upper section while you can edit the Rule Description in the lower section. When you change the Rule Type in the upper section, the various options appearing in the lower section will also change.

Icon Sets Conditional Formatting

Icon sets are another type of conditional formatting that gives an opportunity to create visual effects in your data to see how the value of a cell is compared with the value of other cells. As the name suggests, this feature allows you to put icons in cells based on the values of the cell. Icon sets are quite similar to that of the data bars and color scales. Icon sets make it easy to see how the data values relate to each other. You have a flexibility to choose a desired set of icons from the Icon Sets menu. You can use icons that are most appropriate for the data you are using. Picture 3.3 shows the list of icons available in the icon sets conditional formatting. Perform the following steps to apply the icon sets conditional formatting:

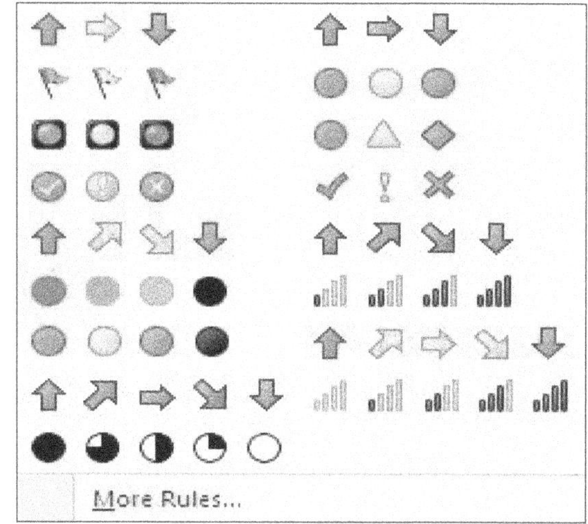

Picture 3.3

1. **Select** some numerical data in the worksheet.

2. Click the **Home** tab, and click the **Conditional Formatting** button under the <u>Styles</u> group. A dropdown list appears.

3. **Move** the mouse pointer and **place** over the <u>Icon Sets</u> category to open a submenu.

4. Click the **More Rules** option in the submenu. The **New Formatting Rule** dialog box appears.

The Format of cells based on their values rule is selected by default. Default values to associate an icon in the cell range appear under the Edit the Rule Description section. You can change these default values according to the data present in the cell range.

5. Type **130** as new value for the <u>Green</u> icon.

6. Type **125** as new value for the <u>Yellow</u> icon.

7. Click the **OK** button after typing the new value.

As the result in your worksheet, the numbers greater than or equal to 130 are indicted by green icon, the number lies between 125 and 130 are indicted by yellow icon, and the number below than 125 are indicated by red icon.

Modifying Rules in Conditional Formatting

The Modifying Rule feature provides the facility to make changes in the rules of conditional formatting. Suppose you have set a rule to a selected data, and it does not seem to be looking good or you want to add some additional rule, then you make changes in the rule by modifying it. For example, the three colors icon set used earlier can be modified by including an additional icon in the rule, and thereafter, display the icon in the cell range. As an example, we will pick the three color icon set used earlier for applying conditional formatting. Perform the following steps to modify the rule:

1. **Select** some data on which you have applied the conditional formatting. In our case, we are using the same data which we had used in previous section.

2. Click the **Home** tab, and click the **Conditional Formatting** button under the <u>Styles</u> group.

3. Click the **Manage Rules** option which opens a **Conditional Formatting Rules Manager** dialog box, as shown in picture 3.4.

The New Rule, Edit Rule, and Delete Rule buttons are used to create a new rule, modify an existing rule, and delete a rule, respectively. Clicking the Show formatting rules for list box displays a list. You can choose an item from the dropdown list to view conditional formatting rules, which you want to apply to currently selected cell range, entire worksheet, or different worksheets in the workbook. The category name of conditional formatting applied on the cell range appears in the dialog box.

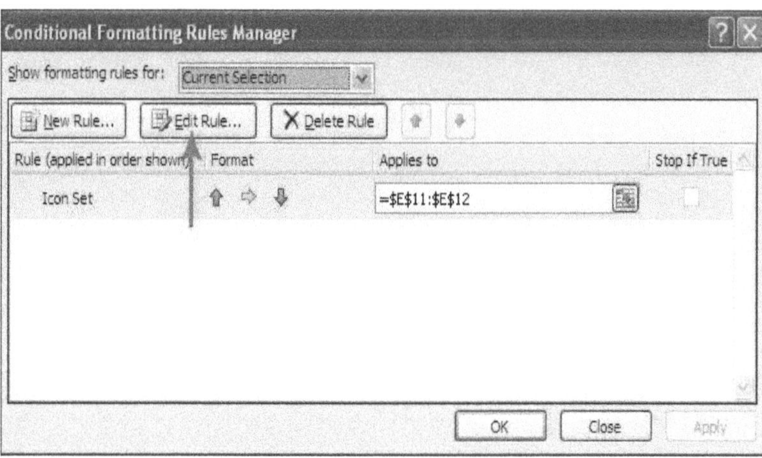

Picture 3.4

4. Click the **Edit Rule** button in the Conditional Formatting Rules Manager dialog box, as shown in picture 3.4 with the red arrow.

It opens the **Edit Formatting Rule** dialog box, as shown in picture 3.5.

5. Click the **Icon Style** list box. Then select the **4 Traffic Lights** option from the dropdown, as shown with the red arrow.

An additional icon appears in the **Icon** list and value for the additional icon is automatically set by Excel on the last icon's value. If required, you can re-type the value in the **Value** text box. However, in our case, we are using the default icon values.

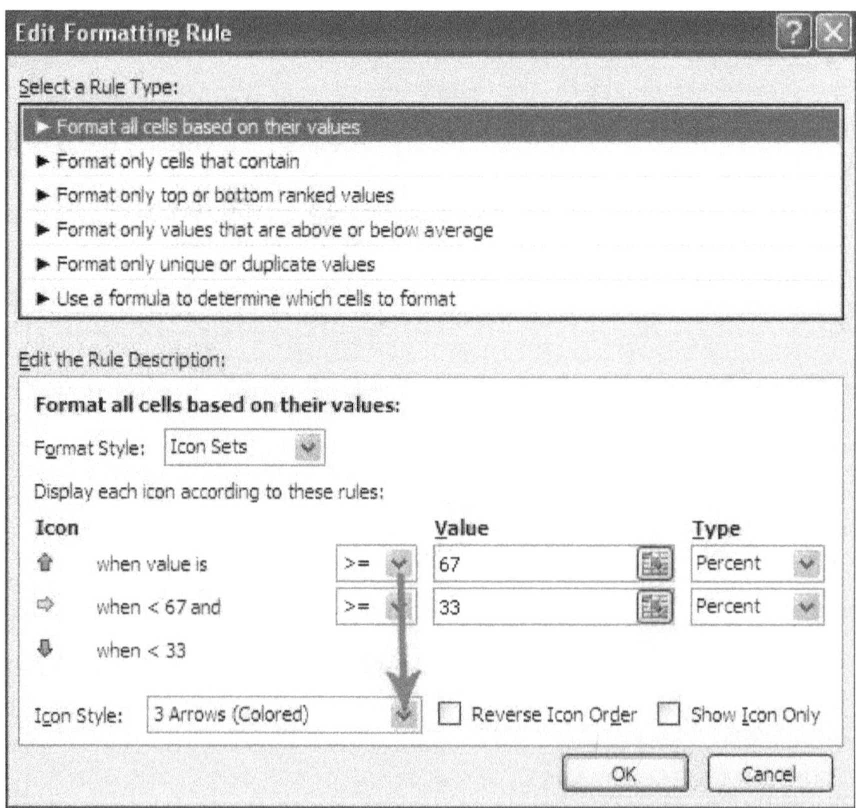

Picture 3.5

6. Click the **OK** button to close the **Edit Formatting Rule** dialog box. The Conditional Formatting Rules Manager dialog box reappears.

7. Click the **Apply** button to implement the modification carried out in the conditional formatting rule.

8. Click the **OK** button to close the Conditional Formatting Rules Manager dialog box. As the result, the worksheet appears with an additional icon included in the conditional formatting rule.

About Sort and Filter Feature

Sort and Filter are the features provided in Excel to arrange and retrieve the specific data. Both the options are present in the same group – Editing group of the Home tab. In Microsoft Excel or any other program, sorting is used to sort the data and display values in ascending or descending form. On the other hand, filtering in Microsoft Excel or any other program filters the data on the basis of the criteria specified by the user and displays only those values, which satisfy the criteria specified by the user.

Sorting Data

Sorting a table in Excel worksheet rearranges the rows based on the content of a particular column. Sometimes, you may want to sort a table to put names in alphabetical order or by some other field present in the worksheet. There are two types of sorting – one is called automatic and the other is custom. The automatic sorting sorts the data in ascending and descending order while the custom sorting sorts and display the data on the basis of condition(s) specified by the user. In this chapter, we will emphasize on custom sorting.

Applying Custom Sorting on Data

As we have already mentioned that in case of Custom Sorting, the sorting is done on the basis of condition(s) specified by the user. In the custom sorting feature, you can select the number of columns on which you want to apply sorting while in other case it is directly applied on the selected column. Perform the following steps to apply custom sorting:

1. **Select** some data from the worksheet. In our case, we have selected the same range on which we earlier applied the Icon set conditional formatting.

2. Click the **Home** tab, and click the **Sort & Filter** button under the Editing group.

3. Click the **Custom Sort** button from the dropdown list. It opens the **Sort** dialog box on the screen.

4. Select the **Column** that you want to sort in the Sort by list box.

5. In the Sort dialog box, click the **Add Level** button at the top-left corner. As the result, one more level is added in the Sort dialog box.

6. **Select** the next column that you want to sort. Then click the **OK** button in the dialog box. The columns of the worksheet are sorted now. You can sort the data based on one column or more than one column. You can also specify the order of data as ascending or descending depending upon your requirement.

Filtering Data

Filtering a data refers to retrieving a specific data, which meets the certain criteria specified by the user. Sometimes you require displaying certain amount of data from the large chunk of data present in a worksheet. In such a case, you can apply filter feature on it. Filtering the data is the best possible way to hide unwanted data from the user without actually deleting it from the hard drive.

Applying Custom Filter on Data

Filtering can be applied on both types of data – text and numeric. In the steps mentioned below, we are applying filter feature on the numeric data, but it can be applied on the text data as well in the same manner. Perform the following steps to learn how to filter data:

1. **Select** a column in which you want to filter the data.

2. Click the **Home** tab, and click the **Sort & Filter** button under the Editing group.

3. Click the **Filter** option from the dropdown list. As the result, a down-arrow button appears on the selected cell in your worksheet, as shown in picture 3.6.

	A	B	C	D	E	F	G
1			CLASS REPORT				
2	▼	▼	MARK ▼	DAVID ▼	CHARLES ▼	KEVIN ▼	
3	SUBJECT	MAX MARKS					
4	ENGLISH	100	70	80	72	67	
5	MATHS	100	57	90	80	82	
6	SCIENCE	100	79	79	85	92	
7	SST	100	60	72	60	87	
8	DRAWING	100	67	80	70	80	
9	G.K. GR.	A+	B	A+	B+	A+	
10	TOTAL	600	$398^{1/2}$	$477^{1/2}$	434	488	
11	% (AGE)		66.30%	79.50%	72.33%	81.33%	
12							
13							

Picture 3.6

4. **Click** the dropdown arrow in your worksheet which is shown in picture 3.6 with the red arrow.

It opens a dropdown list on the screen. This list displays options to sort and filter data. In addition, values under the selected cell (column heading Q4) appear in the list. By un-checking and checking checkboxes of each value, you can hide and re-display the values. The Select All checkbox is used to hide and unhide all the values under a column heading.

Microsoft Excel analyzes the requirement of filters by judging the type of data selected by the user. For example, the name of filter, just above the Select All checkbox, appears automatically on the basis of type data selected for filtering. After analyzing the type of data, Microsoft Excel displays the most relevant and appropriate filter category name for the data.

5. Place the mouse pointer over the **Number Filters** option in the dropdown list. It opens a submenu.

6. Click the **Top 10…** option. It opens the **Top 10 Auto Filter** dialog box.

7. Set the value for **Top** option as **3** in the Top 10 Auto Filter dialog box by clicking the small up-arrow button.

8. Click the **OK** button in the dialog box. As the result, only top three values are visible in your worksheet.

One important point is that whenever the conditional formatting is applied on any one of the column, values present in the other cells corresponding to that column are also affected.

9. Click the **Clear Filter From** option to clear the filter from the worksheet.

Lesson 5
Opening Excel Using Shortcut
Till now, you have to open Microsoft Excel using the Start menu and clicking the Microsoft Excel program again and again. If you perform the steps mentioned below, you can create the keyboard shortcut for Excel of any program. And when you press the shortcut on your keyboard, it will open the program on your screen directly. Perform the following steps to create a shortcut for Microsoft Excel:

1. Click the **Start** button, go to **All Programs**, and click **Microsoft Office**.

2. **Right-click** on Microsoft Excel and select **Properties**. It opens Microsoft Excel Properties dialog box.

3. Click the **Shortcut** tab at the top, and then, **click** in the box beside the **Shortcut Key**.

4. Press **Ctrl+Alt+E** keys together on your keyboard to set the shortcut for Microsoft Excel program.

5. Click the **Apply** and the **OK** button to set the shortcut. Now, when you press Ctrl+Alt+E keys together on your desktop, it will directly open the Microsoft Excel program.

Charts and SmartArt
In this chapter, you learn how to represent data in the form of charts and SmartArts. A chart is the visual representation of numeric values. Charts are often used to compare the data or to show the relationship between the given quantities. The charts can be of various types, such as line chart, column chart, and pie chart. The SmartArt feature of Excel allows you to enhance the appearance of your worksheets by inserting organizational charts in them. Let's first discuss the chart types.

Selecting the Chart Type
You can select a chart type depending on the data to be represented as a chart. The Microsoft Excel provides you with various types of charts to represent your data. For this, you first need to select the data fro the chart and select the type of chart to be used to represent the data. Various types of charts are as follows: Column chart, Bar chart, Line chart, Pie chart, Scatter chart, Area chart, Doughnut chart, Surface chart. Let's now discuss each of chart types in detail.

Column Charts

Column charts display each data point as a vertical column, where the height of a column shows the corresponding values. In the column charts, the value scale is displayed on the vertical axis and they are best suited for comparing data.

Bar Charts

In the bar charts, the data is represented in the form of horizontal bars. The length of the bars corresponds to the value of the data given. A bar chart is a column chart that has been rotated 90 degrees clockwise.

Line Charts

Line charts are used to plot continuous data, that is, each point on a line chart corresponds to a value. A line chart can use any number of data series and you can distinguish the lines by using different colors or line styles. For example, plotting budget and expenses as a line chart may enable you to indentify cost fluctuations.

Pie Charts

Pie charts are used to show relative proportions or contributions to a whole. These charts are most effective while representing a small amount of data. The various sectors or blocks in a pie chart represent data as a proportion of the whole.

Scatter Charts

Scatter charts are used to show the relationship between two variables. The Scatter chart can display better the monthly sale of items and calls made to sell them.

Area Charts

In area charts, areas are used to represent values.

Doughnut Charts

Doughnut charts are used to display more than one series of data. This chart can display better the data with two series – budget and expenses.

Surface Charts

Surface charts are useful when you want to find optimum combinations between two sets of data. You can use a surface chart when both categories and data series are numeric values. After discussing the various chart types, let's learn how to select a particular chart type for any given data in Microsoft Excel.

Selecting the Chart Type

Consider a situation where you have been provided with data and you need to represent that data in form of chart. Let's now perform the following steps to select the appropriate type of chart for representing the data:

1. **Select** the data for which the chart is to be drawn.

2. Click the **Insert** tab, and **select** an appropriate chart type from the various categories of charts under the Charts group.

3. **Click** outside the chart to deselect the chart. After selecting the chart type, let's learn to set the chart options.

Setting the Chart Options

After selecting the appropriate chart type, you can select various chart options for your chart. You can also perform various functions, such as adding and changing the chart and axis title; adding, removing, and positioning the chart legend. A legend is used to identify the various series in a chart. Let's first start with setting the chart title.

Setting the Chart Title

In order to start with setting the chart title, you need to perform the following steps to add a title to your chart to indentify the chart data:

1. **Select** the chart in the Excel worksheet that is to be titled. You can select it by just clicking on it.

2. Click the **Layout** tab, and click the **Chart Title** under the Labels group. It opens a dropdown list on the screen.

3. **Click** on a location to place the chart title in the dropdown list. For example, click the **Above Chart** location to place the chart title at the top of the chart.

4. **Replace** the default chart title text with your own title text by typing a new title. Now, let's learn how to set the axes title in a chart.

Setting the Axes Title

The charts can be two dimensional (2D) or three dimensional (3D). The 2D charts consist of X-axis and Y-axis, where X-axis is the horizontal axis and Y-axis is the vertical axis. On the other hand, the 3D charts have three axes, namely the X, Y, and Z axes. These axes are known as value axes, because they contain the values of the chart drawn. Perform the following steps on your computer to show how to set the axes title:

1. Click the **Layout** tab on the Ribbon.

2. Click the **Axis Titles** button under the Labels group.

3. Place the mouse-pointer over the **Primary Vertical Axis Title** in the dropdown list. It opens a submenu.

4. **Click** the Axis Title position in the submenu. For example, click the **Horizontal Title** position to display axis title in vertical on the chart.

5. **Replace** the default axis title text with your own text by typing your text. Now, let's proceed to set the legends and values in a chart.

Legends and Values

A legend is used in Excel charts to indentify various data series presented in a chart. Data series are the series of data to be displayed in the form of chart. In Excel, charts indentify one data series from another by allocating a unique color or a pattern to them. Perform the following steps to set a legend in a chart:

1. Click the **Layout** tab, and click the **Legend** button under the <u>Labels</u> group.

2. **Click** anywhere in the chart to display legends on chart. For example, click the **Show Legend at Right** option to display legends at the right side of the chart.

As the result, the legends appear on the right side of the chart. Now, let's learn how to resize and reposition charts in an Excel worksheet.

Resizing and Positioning the Charts in a Worksheet

If you think that your chart does not does not fit well in the worksheet, then you can resize or reposition it so that it can be properly placed in the worksheet. You can move and resize your chart with the mouse. Let's now learn how to resize or move a chart.

Resizing a Chart

If you want to change the size of your chart, you need to put the mouse-pointer on any of the eight handles and then drag the mouse to resize the chart. The handles are the black dots that appear on the chart's border when you select it. Perform the following steps to resize a chart:

1. **Click** the border of the chart. Eight handles appear on the border of the chart. You can use these handles to resize the chart.

2. **Move** the mouse-pointer over any of the handles. Then **click** and **drag** the mouse to get the desired size of the chart.

3. **Release** the mouse button and you will get the desired size.

Moving a Chart

Whenever you select a chart style for your data, by default, it appears in the middle of the screen. For quick interpretation, the chart must align with its data in a proper way. Therefore, you need to move the chart to a new location within the worksheet. For that purpose, click the chart's border and drag it to the desired location. Perform the following steps to move a chart:

1. **Click** the border of the chart, and then **place** the mouse-pointer over a handle appearing on the border of chart.

2. **Click** and **drag** the chart to a new location on the worksheet.

3. **Release** the mouse button. As the result, the chart moves to a new position.

Converting a Chart Type into another Type

Microsoft Excel allows you to convert a chart type into another chart type. Perform the following steps on your computer for this:

1. **Click** the border of the chart, and then click the **Design** tab on the Ribbon.

2. Click the **Change Chart Type** button under the <u>Type</u> group. The Change Chart Type dialog box appears with the chart's category name appearing on the left side and various charts available under the category on the right side, as shown in picture 3.7.

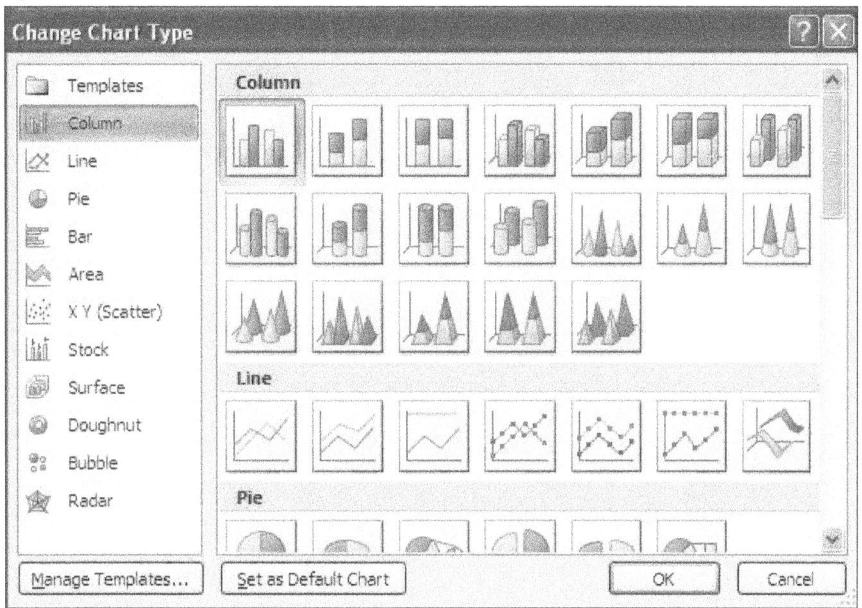

Picture 3.7

3. **Click** on a chart category, say **Column**. Then **select** a chart type.

4. **Click** on a chart type, say **Stacked Column 3-D**, and click the **OK** button. As the result, it changes the type of your chart. Now, let's learn to work with SmartArts.

Working with SmartArts

The SmartArt feature of Excel is used for various types of presentation tasks, such as relationships, illustrating procedural steps, and organizational charts. This feature has replaced the organizational charts feature in Microsoft Office 2007 suite, as it provides a variety of customizable graphic images to choose from. You can make modifications to a SmartArt from the SmartArt Tool's contextual menu.

Inserting SmartArts in a Worksheet

In Microsoft Excel, different types of SmartArts are put under different categories. Whenever you insert a SmartArt, Microsoft Excel displays the name of different categories and preview of SmartArts available under the category. Based upon the nature of the data, (whether it is displaying some sort of relationship, hierarchy, or process) you can select a SmartArt, which best suits your data. Perform the following steps to insert a SmartArt:

1. **Open** MS Excel, and click the **Insert** tab.

2. Click the **SmartArt** button under the <u>Illustrations</u> group.

The **Choose a SmartArt Graphic** dialog box appears on the screen (shown in picture 3.8). The left side displays the name of categories, the middle portion of dialog box displays different SmartArts available under a category, and the right side displays the preview of the selected SmartArt. The various categories of the SmartArt feature are as follows:

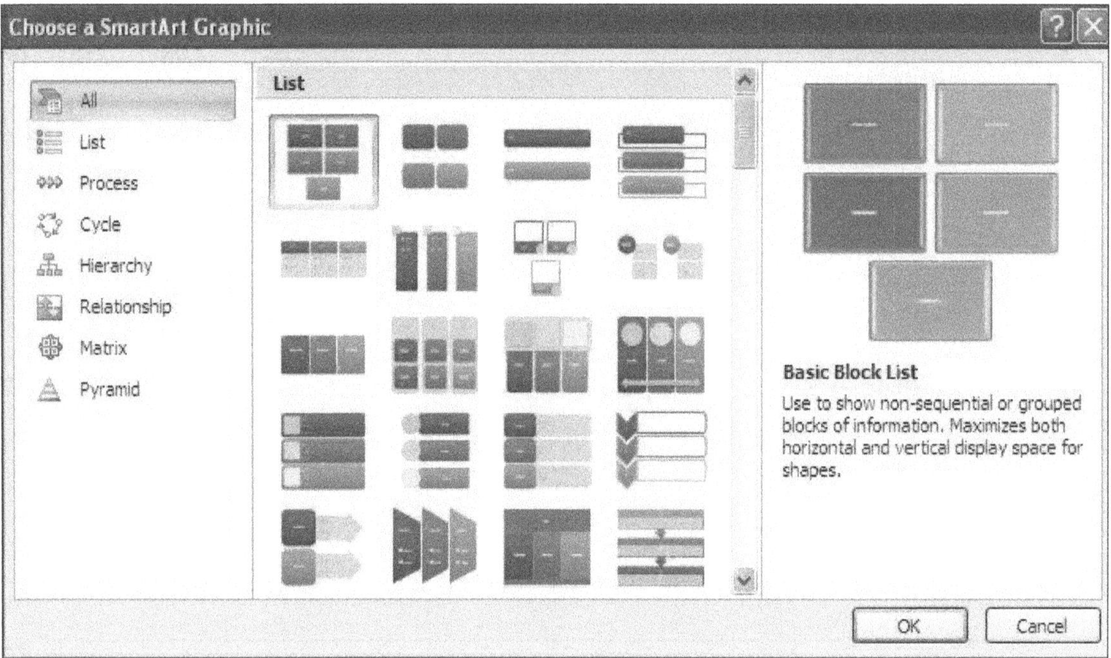

Picture 3.8

- **List:** Creates a list of data in a random order
- **Process:** Represents the task in a sequential order
- **Cycle:** Provides a circular orientation for a correlated task
- **Hierarchy:** Creates organizational charts
- **Relationship:** Shows connections
- **Matrix:** Illustrates the interdependent relationship
- **Pyramid:** Arranges the objects according to their importance

3. **Select** a SmartArt category. In this case, we have selected the **Hierarchy** category. Various SmartArts available under this category appear in the middle portion of the dialog box.

4. **Select** the SmartArt of your choice. In this case, we have selected the **Hierarchy** SmartArt. The preview of the selected SmartArt appears in the rightmost part of the dialog box.

5. Click the **OK** button to add the SmartArt to your worksheet.

Now, you can add text to the blocks of the SmartArt graphic. You can move and resize the graphic by dragging any of the handles along the border.

Adding Text to a SmartArt

You can also add text to the SmartArt that you have inserted into your worksheet. These SmartArts can be used as labels or for the purpose of showing any other relevant information. Perform the following steps to add text to the SmartArt:

1. **Insert** SmartArt graphic into your worksheet using the steps given under the heading 'Inserting SmartArt in a Worksheet'.

2. **Add** the text to your SmartArt graphic by typing in the text pane appearing on the left side of the graphic. You can also type directly into the graphic blocks just by clicking into it.

3. Click the **Add Shape** button in the Create Graphics group under the Design tab to add more blocks into the existing graphic.

4. **Select** the position of the block, and **type** the text into the block.

The buttons in the Shapes group, under the Format tab, offer various ways to modify the shape and size of your graphics. However, their functionality depends on the particular graphic you are using. After learning the process of inserting a SmartArt and adding details into it, let's now proceed to modify the default shape of a SmartArt by applying a style on it.

Selecting a Style of SmartArt

You can change the appearance of a SmartArt by applying a new style, color, and layout to it. When you are in the process of changing the appearance of a SmartArt, MS Excel ensures that the hierarchy level in the SmartArt does not get disturbed or changed. For applying different styles to your graphics, you can use the SmartArt Tool's contextual menu under the Design tab. Perform the following steps and learn to change the appearance of the SmartArt that we have created earlier in the chapter:

1. **Select** the SmartArt graphic by clicking on its boundary.

2. Click the **Design** tab. In case you want to change the style of a SmartArt, then select a style for your graphic under the **SmartArt Styles** group.

3. Click the **Change Colors** button under the SmartArt Styles group to change the color of your graphic.

4. **Select** a color scheme in the dropdown list that appears. As the result, the selected color is applied to your graphic.

Converting a SmartArt to a Hyperlink

A hyperlink allows a user to instantly access another place in the workbook, browse to another workbook, a Web page, or any other location. When you click the cell or the SmartArt graphic that contains the Hyperlink function, MS Excel opens the file stored at that particular location. Perform the following steps to link a SmartArt graphic to a Web page:

1. **Select** the SmartArt, and click the **Insert** tab.

2. Click the **Hyperlink** button under the <u>Links</u> group. It opens the Insert Hyperlink dialog box on the screen.

3. **Select** the location for which you want to create the link under the <u>Link to</u> option. In this case, we have selected the **Existing File or Web Page** option.

4. **Type** the address of the link beside the Address option. For example, you can type http://www.facebook.com/cromosys

5. Finally, click the **OK** button to confirm all the changes.

Lesson 6
Functions in Excel
Function is a predefined formula that performs calculations by using specific values in a particular order. The values used in the function are called arguments, which must appear in a specific order. For example, the average function is used to calculate the average of several values or arguments.

The functions are used to perform computation in an easy manner. For example, calculating the sum of several cells, if done manually, is quite difficult and time consuming process; however, with the help of the SUM function, such a task can be completed quickly without spending much time and effort. One point to remember is that functions work on a specific range, means without specifying a range you cannot use a function. A function requires a starting range and an ending range.

There is a specific syntax for writing any function. You have to write the function in address bar in a proper syntax; otherwise, the function will not work. In this chapter, you learn about the basic of a function, in which you learn about function syntax, necessary information for a function, correcting error in a function, and copying the function. Next, you explore the arithmetical function, in which you learn about the SUM, Average, and Count functions. Thereafter, you study about the text function, where you learn about the FIND, REPLACE, and CONCATENATE functions. At the end, we discuss about the financial function, where you learn about the PMT, PV, RATE, DURATION, YIELD, and DOLLARDE functions. Let's begin with the basics of a function.

Defining Basics of a Function
While using functions to perform an operation, the function must include syntax of the function, and arguments passed in the function. If we do not use the proper syntax or we pass the incorrect argument, the function occurs with an error in the result. Let's discuss the function syntax in the next section.

Explaining the Function Syntax
A function begins with the equal sign (=) followed by the function's name and its arguments. The function name tells Excel what calculation to perform. The arguments are present inside round brackets. For example, the most used function in Excel is the SUM function, which is used to add various data in selected cells. The SUM function is written as:

=SUM (A1:A9)
This function adds the contents of cell range A1 to A9.

Getting Required Information for a Function

It is very difficult to remember the syntax of each function present in Microsoft Excel. To assist the user, Microsoft Excel provides Excel help, which the user can use to know about the syntax and usage of a function. Perform the following steps to understand how to seek help on any function:

1. Click the **Insert Function** button beside the Formula bar, as shown in picture 3.9 with the red arrow numbered 1.

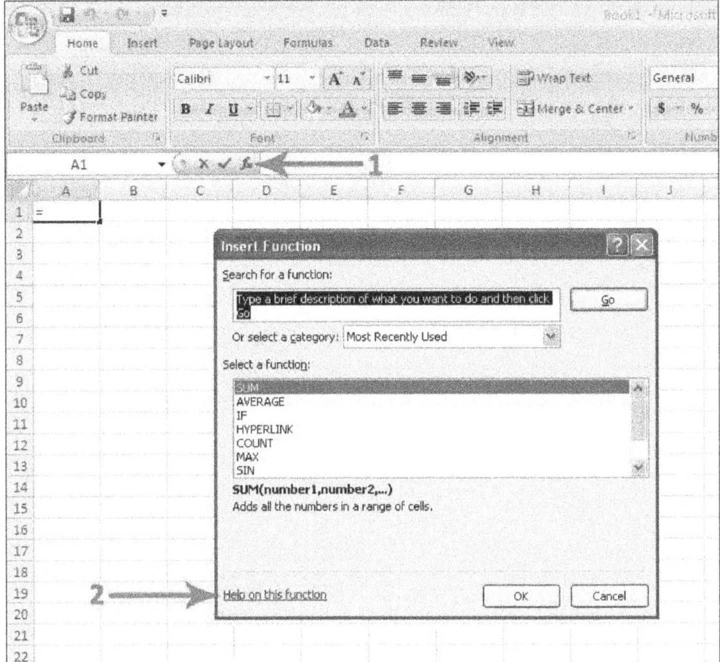

Picture 3.9

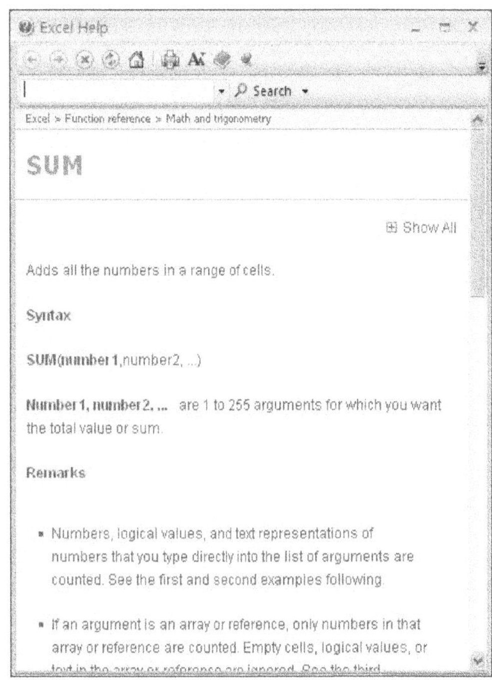

Picture 4.0

It opens the **Function Arguments** dialog box on your computer screen, which is shown in the middle of picture 3.9.

2. Click the **Help on this function** link in the Function Arguments dialog box, as shown in picture 3.9 with the red arrow numbered 2.

It opens the **Excel Help** window over the Function Argument dialog box, as shown in picture 4.0. You can use the Excel Help window to get all necessary information over the SUM function.

The Function Arguments dialog box contains the information regarding the selected function. In our case, it is showing basic information related to the SUM function, such as what the function is all about, syntax of the function.

Correcting Errors in a Function

Judging an error in a function is not a tough job. Sometimes, when you enter a function in a Formula bar, Excel displays a value that begins with a hash mark (#). This is a signal, which tells us that the formula is giving an error value and you need to correct the formula to remove this error. However, if the entire cell is filled with hash-mark characters, this means the column is not wide enough to display the resulted value. You can either increase the column width or change the number format of the cell. Types of error values that may appear in a cell having a formula are given as follows:

#DIV/0!: Divides some value by zero. This also occurs when the formula attempts to divide by an empty cell (means a cell that has no value).
#NAME?: Uses a name that Excel does not know. This can happen if you delete a name that is used in the formula.
#N/A: Refers (directly or indirectly) to a cell that uses the NA function to signal that data is not available. Some functions, such as VLOOKUP can also return #N/A.
#NULL!: Uses an intersection of two ranges that does not intersect.
#NUM!: Occurs with invalid numeric value in a function. For example, you assign a negative value where a positive value is expected.
#REF!: Refers to an invalid cell. This can happen if the cell has been deleted from the worksheet.
#VALUE!: Includes an argument or operand of the wrong type. An operand is a value or cell reference that a formula uses to calculate a result.

There are different errors, which appear after writing a function. Now after judging the errors, they must be removed to get the desired output. If there is an error in a function, then double click the cell having function or select the cell and the function will appear in the address bar where you can make changes.

Copying the Function
Sometimes, you need to apply the same function multiple times. In such situations, it is a time consuming process to type the same function repeatedly. To solve this problem, you can copy the function and use it wherever you want. Perform the following steps to understand how a Copy Function works:

1. **Open** a worksheet and **enter** some data in it.

2. **Select** a cell in which you want to get output. Then **click** the **Insert Function** button near <u>Format bar</u>. It opens the Insert Function dialog box.

3. **Select** a desired function from the <u>Select a function</u> listbox. In our case, we select the **SUM** option.

4. Click the **OK** button in the dialog box. It opens the **Function Arguments** dialog box on the screen.

5. **Select** the range in the column beside **Number1** whose data you want to add. In our case, we select B3:F3 cell.

6. Click the **OK** button. All the numbers are added, and the output appears in the G3 cell.

7. Click the **Copy** button in the standard toolbar. A blinking margin surrounds the cell address **G3**, indicating that its formula has been copied.

8. **Select** the cell where you want to paste the formula, and then click the **Paste** button in the standard toolbar. In our case, we select **G4** cell. Similarly, you can apply the Copy Function on rest of the cells.

Using Arithmetical Functions

The arithmetical functions are used to perform the different arithmetic calculations. MS Excel is aware of basic algebraic functions, such as addition (+), subtraction (-), multiplication (*), and division (/). Some of the basic functions used in MS Excel are:

Sum Function: Calculates the total value in the selected range of cells.
Average Function: Calculates the average or the mean value of a group of numbers.
Count: Counts the number of numeric values in a specified range of cells.

The SUM Function

The SUM function is the most basic and one of the most popular functions used in MS Excel. In Algebra, it is used to get the addition of two or more numbers; whereas, in MS Excel, it is used to add the contents of various cells and the result is displayed in the active cell containing the formula. The syntax for the addition of two numbers is

=SUM(number1, number2)
where, **number1** and **number2** are the numbers that you want to add.

In case you want to add a range of selected cells for the data, then (for example) the syntax can be: =SUM(B3:B8). Here, the selected range of cells is B3 to B8 and the result is displayed in the cell containing the formula. Now perform the following steps to use MS Excel's SUM function directly into your worksheet:

1. Click the **Formulas** tab at the top in the Excel window.

2. Click the down arrow button of the **AutoSum** option in the Function Library group.

3. Click the **Sum** option from the dropdown list.

It displays the sum of selected cells directly after the selected cells, shown in picture 4.1. You can also widen the range of selected cells as per your requirement.

It displays the result of the formula in the cell B9. After learning the SUM function, let's learn about the Average function.

Picture 4.1

The Average Function

The Average function calculates the average or mean value of the group of numbers. The calculation of the average function involves the sum of all the numbers divided by the number of the values. The syntax for this function is:

=AVERAGE(Number1, Number2, Number3, Number4, ……… .)

Perform the following steps to apply the Average function to calculate average of a group of numbers:

1. Click the down arrow button of the **AutoSum** option in the Function Library group.

2. Click the **Average** option from the dropdown list.

It displays the average of selected cells directly after the selected cells. You can also widen the range of selected cells as per your requirements. The result of the formula in the cell B9 is displayed in the same cell. Another example for calculating average in MS Excel is:

=AVERAGE(4, B3:B5)

This formula is evaluated as the average of constant value 4 with the values stored in the cells B3, B4, and B5.

Any of these functions can take other functions as argument. For example,
=SUM(A2:A4, AVERAGE(C3:C5))

This formula first finds the average of the values in the cells C3, C4, C5, and then, this average will add to the sum of A2, A3, and A4. After learning the Average function, let's learn about the Count function.

The Count Function
The Count function counts the number of cells that contains numbers in the range or group of cells. Perform the following steps to count the number of cells by applying the Count function:

1. Click the down arrow button of the **AutoSum** option in the Function Library group.

2. Click the **Count Numbers** option from the dropdown list.

It displays the number of values in the selected cells directly after the selected range of cells. You can also widen the range of selected cells as per your requirements. The number of values in the selected range will be displayed in the cell containing the formula. In our data, the number of numeric values is six. After learning about the arithmetical functions, let's learn about the text functions.

Using Text Functions
The text function is used to convert the values of the cells to a prescribed text format. Most of the text functions can be easily accessed in the Function Library group under the Formula tab. Some of them are described as follows:

FIND: Helps in finding one text value within another
REPLACE: Replaces the character within text
CONCATENATE: Joins several text items into one

The FIND Function
The FIND function is used to locate one text string within a second text string, and return the number of the starting position of the first text string from the first character of the second text string. This function is case sensitive and is intended to use with single-byte character set.

The FIND function always counts each character, whether single byte or double-byte, as one, depending on the default language setting of your computer. The syntax for this function is:

=FIND(find_text,within_text,start_num)
where,

Find_text: Refers to the text that you want to find.
Within_text: Refers to the text containing the text that you want to find.
Start_num: Refers t the character at which you need to start the search. The first character in Within_text is character number 1. If you omit Start_num, it is assumed to be 1.

The REPLACE Function

The REPLACE function replaces a part of the text string with a different text string. Replacing the text string is based on the number of characters and the number of bytes specified. The REPLACE function always counts each character, whether single byte or double-byte, as one, depending on the default language setting of your computer. The syntax for this function is:

=REPLACE(old_text,start_num,num_chars,new_text)
where,

Old_text: Refers to the text in which you want to replace some characters.
Start_num: Denotes the position of the character in old_text that you want to replace with new_text.
Num_chars: Refers to the number of characters in old_text that you want **REPLACES** to replace with new_text.
New_text: Denotes the text that will replace characters in old_text. Now, perform the following steps to learn the Replace function practically:

1. Type: **Look** in the cell B3 of your Excel worksheet. We will replace the word 'Look' with 'Book' using Replace function.

2. **Click** to select the cell B4 in your Excel worksheet. Then click the **Insert Function** button beside the Formula bar which opens the Insert Function dialog box.

3. **Type** the name of the function you are looking for in the **Search for a function** column. In our case, we type **REPLACE**.

4. Click the **OK** button in the dialog box. It opens the **Function Arguments** dialog box on the screen, as shown in picture 4.2.

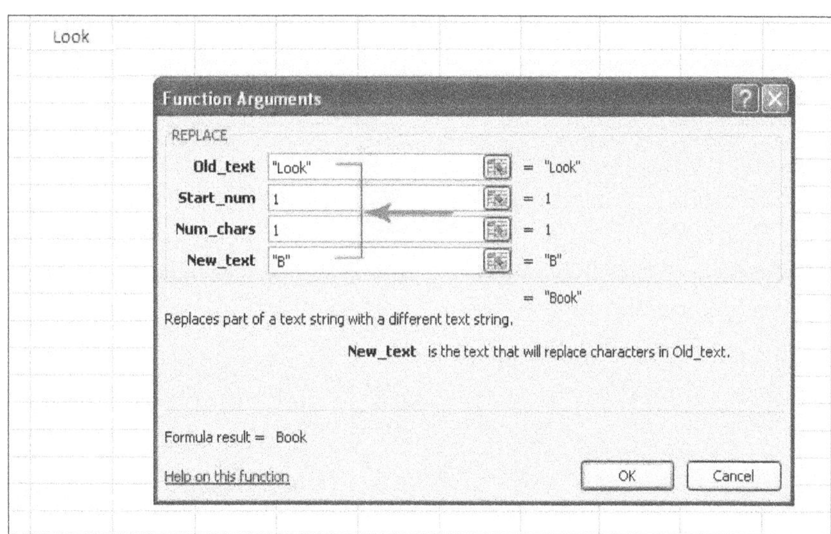

Picture 4.2

5. **Type** the values beside the respective options. In our case, we type: **"Look"** in the Old_text textbox, as shown in picture 4.2. Type: **1** in the Start_num textbox, type: **1** in the Next_chars textbox, and type: **"B"** in the New_text textbox respectively.

6. Click the **OK** button at the bottom. As the result, the old_text "Look" is replaced by the new_text "Book" in the selected cell.

The CONCATENATE Function

The CONCATENATE function is used to join two or more text strings into a single text string in the Excel worksheet. The items to be joined could be text strings, numbers, or single-cell references. The syntax for the function is:

=CONCATENATE(text1, text2, ...)
where,

text1, text2, ... are 1 to 255 text items to be joined into a single text item.

For example, if you want to join the text in the B3, B4, C4, and B5 (as shown in picture 4.3), then the concatenated text will be displayed in the selected B7 cell. Let's perform the following steps to use the Concatenate function:

1. Click the **Insert Function** button beside the Formula bar. The Insert function dialog box appears on the screen.

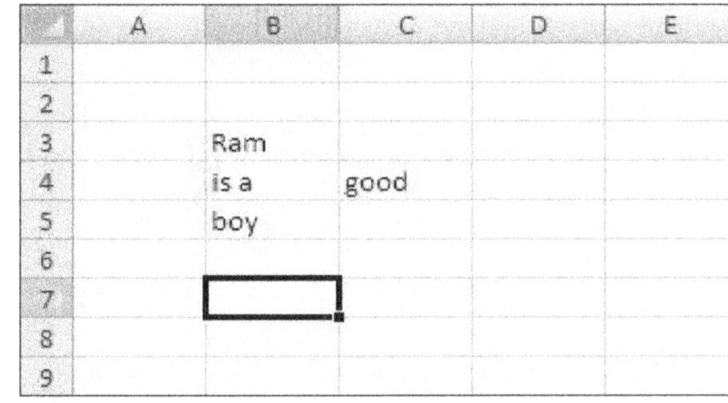
Picture 4.3

2. **Type** the name of the function you are looking for in the Search for a function column. In our case, we type **CONCATENATE**.

3. Click the **OK** button to open the **Function Arguments** dialog box. Then **type** the values in their respective columns. In our case, we type **B3** in the Text1 textbox, **B4** in the Text2 textbox, **C4** in the Text3 textbox, and **B5** in the Text4 textbox respectively, as shown in picture 4.4.

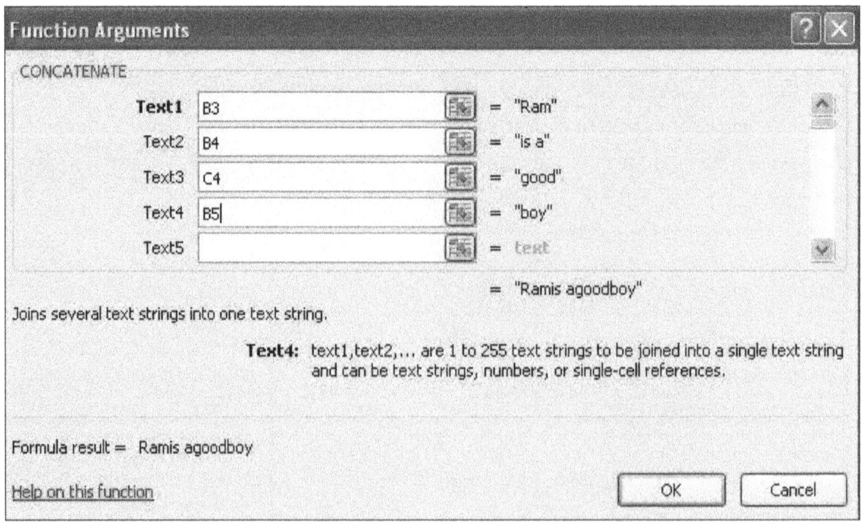
Picture 4.4

4. Click the **OK** button in the dialog box. The CONCATENATED text is displayed in the active cell B7, as shown in picture 4.5.

You can also use ampersand (&) operator in place of the CONCATENATE function; the results are same for both the functions. For example, the formula **=B3&B4&C4&B5** and **=CONCATENATE(B3,B4,C4,B5)** will yield the same results.

The output gets displayed in the cell containing the formula. After learning the use of text function, let's learn about the financial functions.

Picture 4.5

Lesson 7
Using Financial Functions
Microsoft Excel provides a series of functions used to perform various types of finance related operations. These functions use common factors depending on the value that is being calculated. Some of these functions deal with investment or loan financing. Now, let's discuss some of the major financial functions:

The PMT Function
The PMT function is used to calculate the payment for a loan based on constant payments and a constant interest rate. The syntax for this function is:

=PMT(rate,nper,pv,fv,type)
where,

Rate: Refers to the rate of interest for the loan.
Nper: Refers to the total number of payments for the loan.
Pv: Denotes the present value, which is the total amount that a series of future payments is worth now.
Fv: Refers to the future value or a cash balance that you want to attain after the last payment is made. If this Fv is left blank, then the future value of the loan will be considered as zero.
Type: Denotes a logical value, which can be payments at the beginning of the period = 1, payments at the end of the period = 0. If required, then Type can be left blank or omitted.

Consider a case, where you need to calculate the monthly payment for a loan on Rs 12000.00 with 5% rate of interest for 10 months, as shown in picture 4.6. So, perform the following steps to calculate the monthly payment based on the data given in the picture:

1. Click the **Formulas** tab at the top in the Excel window. Then **click** the arrow button of the <u>Financial</u> option in the Function Library group.

2. Choose the **PMT** option from the dropdown list. It opens the **Function Arguments** dialog box on the screen.

Picture 4.6

3. **Type** the values in their respective columns. In our case, we type **A3/12** in the Rate textbox, **A4** in the Nper textbox, and **A2** in the Pv textbox respectively (shown in picture 4.7). Here, the rate of interest is divided by 12 to get the monthly rate.

4. Click the **OK** button in the dialog box. As the result, Excel will display value in the selected cell, which is the monthly payment for a loan with the given values in the cells A3, A4, and A5, respectively.

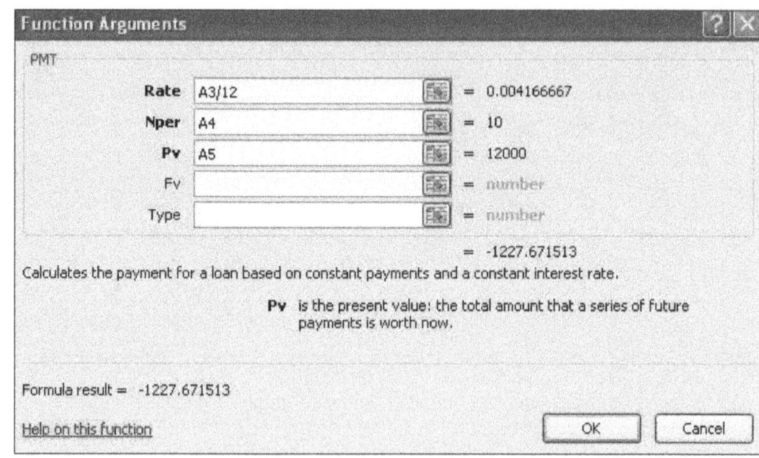

Picture 4.7

The PV Function

The PV function returns the present value of an investment, which is based on the interest rate and a constant payment schedule. The syntax for the functions is:

=PV(rate,nper,pmt,fv,type),
where,

Rate: Refers to the rate of interest per period.
Nper: Implies the total number of payments in an annuity.
Pmt: Denotes an amount paid at the fixed interval of time (majored in months or year). It includes Principal amount and rate of interest.
Fv: Refers to the future value, or a cash balance that you want to attain after the last payment is made. If Fv is left blank, then the future value of loan will be considered zero.
Type: Denotes a logical value, which can be payments at the beginning of the period = 1, payments at the end of the period = 0. If required, then Type can be left blank or omitted.

Consider a situation where you need to calculate the present value (PV) for Rs. 500.00, the amount paid out of an insurance annuity at the end of every month with 8% rate of interest for 20 years, as shown in picture 4.8. Perform the following steps to calculate the present value on the basis of data given in the picture:

1. Click the arrow button of the **Financial** option in the Function Library group of the Formulas tab.

2. Choose the **PV** option from the dropdown list. It opens the **Function Arguments** dialog box.

Picture 4.8

3. **Type** the values in their respective columns. In our case, we type **A3/12** in the Rate textbox, **12*A4** in the Nper textbox, and **A5** in the Pmt textbox respectively (picture 4.9).

4. Click the **OK** button in the dialog box. The rate of interest is divided by 12 to get the monthly rate, and the annual amount is multiplied by 12 to get the total payment to be made by the customer.

Now the selected cell A5 will show the present value of an annuity with the values given in the cells A2, A3, and A4, respectively. After learning the PV function, let's learn about the RATE function.

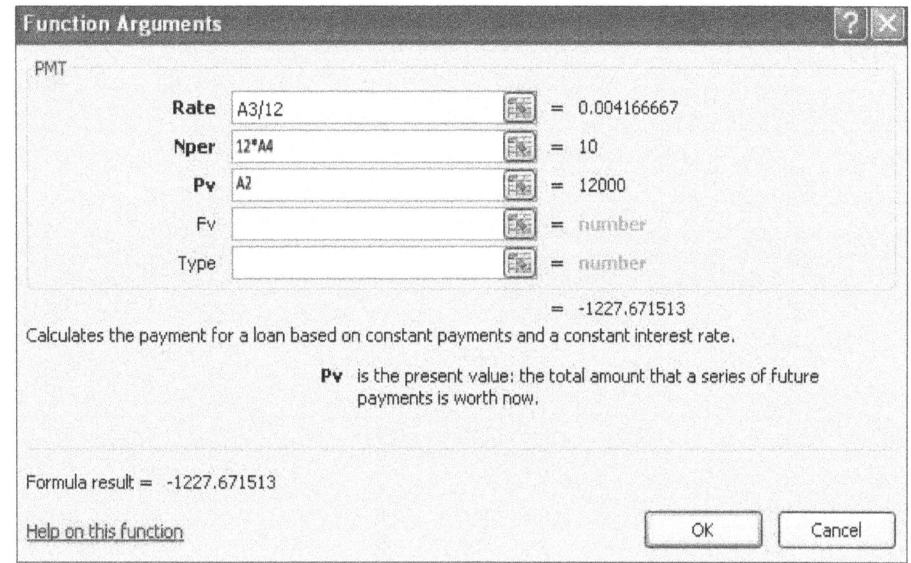

Picture 4.9

The RATE Function
The RATE function returns the rate of interest per period of an annuity. It can have zero or more solution and is calculated by iteration. The syntax for the function is

=RATE(nper,pmt,pv,fv,type,guess)
where,

Nper: Refers to the total number of payment periods in an annuity.
Pmt: Denotes an amount, which is paid at the fixed interval of time (majored in months or year). It includes Principal and rate of interest.
Pv: Refers to the present value, which is the total amount that a series of future payments is worth now.
Fv: Denotes the future value, or a cash balance that you want to attain after the last payment is made. If Fv is left blank, then the future value of loan will be considered as zero.
Type: Denotes a logical value, which can be payments at the beginning of the period =1, payments at the end of the period =0. If required, then Type can be left blank or omitted.
Guess: Refers to the guess for the rate of interest. If you omit guess, it is assumed to be 10%. RATE usually converges if guess is between 0 and 1.

Now, let's suppose that you need to calculate the rate of interest for the amount Rs. 8000.00 with the monthly payment for Rs. 200 for 4 years. Perform the following steps to calculate the rate of interest on the basis of this data:

1. Click the arrow button of the **Financial** option in the Function Library group of the Formulas tab.

2. Choose the **RATE** option from the dropdown list. It opens the Function Arguments dialog box.

3. **Type** the values in their respective columns. In our case, we type **12*D2** in the Nper textbox, **D3** in the Pmt textbox, and **D4** in the Pv textbox, respectively.

4. Click the **OK** button in the dialog box. The number of years of the loan is multiplied by 12 to get the number of months.

The selected cell A5 in your worksheet will represent the monthly rate of the loan with the given values in the cells D2, D3, and D4, respectively. After learning the RATE function, let's learn about the DURATION function.

The DURATION Function
The DURATION function returns the annual duration of a security with periodic interest payments. The syntax of the DURATION function is given as follows:

=DURATION(settlement,maturity,coupon,yld,frequency,basis)
where,

Settlement: Refers to the security settlement date.
Maturity: Denotes the security maturity date.
Coupon: Refers to the coupon rate.
Yld: Denotes the security's annual yield.
Frequency: Refers to the number of coupon payments per year.
Basis: Represents the time period, where 1 is considered for annual payments, 2 for semiannual payments, and 4 for quarterly payments. Perform these steps to use the DURATION function:

1. **Open** a new worksheet and **enter** required data in it, as shown in picture 5.0.

2. **Select** the cell on which you want to apply DURATION function. In our case, we select B7 cell.

3. Click the arrow button of the **Financial** option in the Function Library group of the Formula tab.

	A	B	C	D
1				
2	Sattlement Date	30-Oct-07		
3	Maturity Date	30-Dec-07		
4	Percent Coupon	8		
5	Percent Yield	9		
6	Frequency	2		
7	Basis	1		
8				
9				

Picture 5.0

4. Click the **DURATION** function from the dropdown list. It opens the Function Arguments dialog box.

5. **Type** the values in their respective columns. In our case, we type **B2** in the Settlement, **B3** in the Maturity, **B4** in the Coupon, **B5** in the Yld, **B6** in the Frequency, and **B7** in the Basis textbox, respectively (picture 5.1).

6. Click the **OK** button in the dialog box. The output appears on the worksheet.

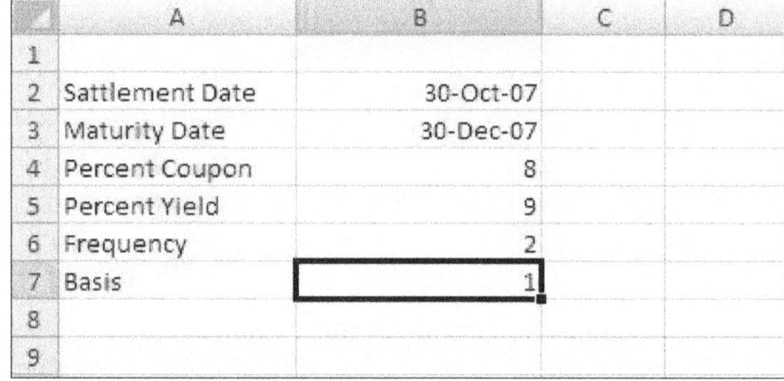

Picture 5.1

The YIELD Function

The YIELD function returns the yield on a security that pays periodic interest. The syntax of the function is given as follows:

=YIELD(settlement,maturity,rate,pr,redemption,frequency,basis)

In this syntax, Pr is used for price, redemption is a security's redemption value, and other terms are already discussed in the previous functions. Now perform the following steps to learn to use the YIELD function:

1. **Open** a new worksheet and **enter** required data in it, as shown in picture 5.2.

2. **Select** the cell on which you want to apply YIELD function. In our case, we select B8 cell.

3. Click the arrow button of the **Financial** option in the Function Library group of the Formulas tab.

4. Click the **YIELD** option from the dropdown list. It opens the Function Arguments dialog box.

	A	B
1		
2	Settlement Date	30-Oct-07
3	Maturity Date	30-Dec-07
4	Percent Coupon(Rate)	5.75%
5	Price(Pr)	95.04287
6	Redemption Value	100
7	Frequency	2
8	Basis	0
9		

Picture 5.2

5. **Type** the values in their respective columns. In our case, we type **B2** in the Settlement textbox, **B3** in Maturity, **B4** in Rate, **B5** in Pr, **B6** in Redemption, **B7** in Frequency, and **B8** in Basis, respectively, as shown in picture 5.3.

6. Click the **OK** button in the dialog box.

The output appears on the worksheet, and function syntax appears in the Formula bar.

Function Arguments

YIELD

Settlement	B2	= 39385
Maturity	B3	= 39446
Rate	B4	= 0.0575
Pr	B5	= 95.04287
Redemption	B6	= 100

= 0.366057649

Returns the yield on a security that pays periodic interest.

Redemption is the security's redemption value per $100 face value.

Formula result = 0.366057649

Help on this function

OK   Cancel

Picture 5.3

The DOLLARDE Function

The DOLLARDE function is used to convert a dollar price expressed as a function into a dollar price expressed as a decimal number. The following is the syntax to write the DOLLARDE function:

=DOLLARDE(fractional_dollar,fraction)

In this syntax, fractional_dollar is a number expressed as a fraction while fraction is the integer to use in a denominator of the fraction.

The following example helps us to understand how the function works:
=DOLLARDE(1.03,26) converts 1.03, read as 1 and 3/26, to a decimal number (1.115).
=DOLLARDE(1.1, 53) converts 1.1, read as 1 and 10/53, to a decimal number (1.1886).

Niranjan Jha Showman
Trainer, Author, Physician, Entrepreneur, Filmmaker, Activist
Cromosys Corporation
Education and Technology Research Center
www.facebook.com/cromosys
+91-9561450045
Nallasopara (W), Mumbai, India

NIRANJAN JHA SHOWMAN

Founder - Niranjan Jha Showman

Education and Technology Research Center

Patankar Park, Nallasopara (W), Mumbai. +91-9561450045

Education, Technology, Publication, Healthcare, Newsmedia, Realtor, Filmmaking

www.facebook.com/cromosys

Cromosys Publication
Teach
Yourself
German
NIRANJAN JHA SHOWMAN

Cromosys Publication
Teach
Yourself
French
NIRANJAN JHA SHOWMAN

Cromosys Publication
Teach
Yourself
Spanish
NIRANJAN JHA SHOWMAN

Cromosys Publication

English
Voice
Accent and
Pronunciation

NIRANJAN JHA SHOWMAN

Teach
Yourself
Autodesk
MAYA
Cromosys Publication
NIRANJAN JHA SHOWMAN

Cromosys Publication
Teach
Yourself
Autodesk
3ds Max
NIRANJAN JHA SHOWMAN

Cromosys Publication
CRIMINAL FACTORY
NIRANJAN JHA SHOWMAN

Cromosys Publication
FOCAL DISASTER
NIRANJAN JHA SHOWMAN

Cromosys Publication
Your talents will not help you succeed without your skill of using them.
NIRANJAN JHA SHOWMAN
BE
MILLIONAIRE
LIKE
ME

Copyright Office
Government of India

सत्यमेव जयते

Extracts
from the Register
of Copyrights

Dated : 22/07/2022

1.	Registration Number	:	**T-83782-2022**
2.	Name, address and nationality of the applicant	:	**NIRANJAN JHA SHOWMAN, CROMOSYS PUBLICATION, 001, JAYSATYAM, PATANKAR ROAD, NALLASOPARA (W), MUMBAI, MAHARASHTRA - 401203. INDIAN**
3.	Nature of the applicant's interest in the copyright of the work	:	**AUTHOR**
4.	Class and description of the work	:	**LITERARY / BOOK**
5.	Title of the work	:	**Teach Yourself Microsoft Excel**
6.	Language of the work	:	**ENGLISH**
7.	Name, address and nationality of the author and if the author is deceased, date of his decease	:	**NIRANJAN JHA SHOWMAN, CROMOSYS PUBLICATION, 001, JAYSATYAM, PATANKAR ROAD, NALLASOPARA (W), MUMBAI, MAHARASHTRA - 401203. INDIAN**
8.	Whether the work is published or unpublished	:	**UNPUBLISHED**
9.	Year and country of first publication and name, address and nationality of the publisher	:	**N.A.**
10.	Years and countries of subsequent publications, if any, and names, addresses and nationalities of the publishers	:	**N.A.** **SAME AS ABOVE**
11.	Names, addresses and nationalities of the owners of various rights comprising the copyright in the work and the extent of rights held by each, together with particulars of assignments and licences, if any	:	
12.	Names, addresses and nationalities of other persons, if any, authorised to assign or licence of rights comprising the copyright	:	**N.A.**
13.	If the work is an 'Artistic work', the location of the original work, including name, address and nationality of the person in possession of the work. (In the case of an architectural work, the year of completion of the work should also be shown).	:	**N.A.**
14.	If the work is an 'Artistic work', whether it is registered under the Designs Act 2000 if yes give details.	:	**N.A.**
15.	If the work is an 'Artistic work', capable of being registered as a design under the Designs Act 2000.whether it has been applied to an article though an industrial process and ,if yes ,the number of times it is reproduced.	:	**N.A.**
16.	Remarks, if any	:	

Diary Number :   **8623/2020-DF/T**
Date of Application :   **25/07/2020**
Date of Receipt :   **25/07/2020**

DEPUTY REGISTRAR OF COPYRIGHTS